# BUSINESS
# AND
# INDUSTRY

The Information Revolution

# BUSINESS
# AND
# INDUSTRY

WALTER OLEKSY

☑® Facts On File, Inc.
AN INFOBASE HOLDINGS COMPANY

Business and Industry

Facts On File, Inc.
11 Penn Plaza
New York, NY 10001

**Library of Congress Cataloging-in-Publication Data**

Oleksy, Walter G., 1930–
   Business and industry / Walter Oleksy.
     p.  cm. — (The Information revolution)
   Includes bibliographical references and index.
   Summary: Surveys the ways in which electronic technology including laptop and portable "powerbook" computers, supercomputers, modems, and videophones have altered work and production.
   ISBN 0-8160-3075-8 (alk. paper)
   1. Business—Data processing—Juvenile literature.  2. Industries—Data processing—Juvenile literature.  3. Information technology—Juvenile literature.  [1. Business—Data processing.  2. Information technology.]  I. Title.  II. Series.
   HF5548.2.0443  1996
   650'.0285—dc20                          96-20415

Text design by Catherine Hyman
Cover design by Nora Wertz

This book is printed on acid-free paper.

Printed in the United States of America

MP FOF 10 9 8 7 6 5 4 3 2 1

# CONTENTS

# INTRODUCTION

## YOU AND THE
## INFORMATION REVOLUTION

A merican business, industry, government, and education have already become actively engaged in a new information revolution proposed and encouraged by President Bill Clinton and Vice President Al Gore shortly after their inauguration early in 1993. They call the new technological concept an "electronic data superhighway," a vast communications system designed to revolutionize data gathering and distribution. Similar in concept to telephone lines that link phone users along a "telephone superhighway," fiber-optic telephone lines or satellite transmission link computers in homes, schools, businesses, banks, research centers, universities, libraries, hospitals, and other outlets by two-way interactive multimedia data, sound, and video.

The Clinton administration wants the United States to take the lead in developing and producing new technology to implement the data superhighway. It could revitalize industry, stimulate the economy, and put the United States in the forefront of worldwide technological competitiveness. The ambitious vision calls for using government-backed research projects, tax incentives, and trade policy to help high-tech industries become engines of economic growth and job creation.

The data superhighway would bring America into direct competition with Japan, France, Germany, and other nations seeking an edge in the technology race, and put more Americans back to work in skilled, high-paying jobs. By enhancing the gathering and dissemination of information, it would have far-reaching effects in education and learning, business and industry, science and medicine, and entertainment, and other fields.

Students could use home or school computers to access distant databases at universities and other institutions, thus enabling them to work with educators in other cities and countries and to communicate and interact with educational materials displayed as integrated text, sound, and video on computers or televisions.

Businesses could send computer drawings and other information between distant points to speed the design and manufacture of new products. Advanced teleconferencing, linking computers with telephones, video recorders, and television sets can enable business and industry to conduct electronic meetings of people in distant cities, and similarly link classrooms with university lecture halls, museums, and libraries.

> The data superhighway would bring America into direct competition with Japan, France, Germany, and other nations seeking an edge in the technology race, and put more Americans back to work in skilled, high-paying jobs.

Scientists and researchers would be able to exchange vast amounts of written, audio, and visual data regardless of where they were located, working together more efficiently and achieving greater shared knowledge, thus speeding up otherwise lengthy research projects and avoiding duplication of study.

Individuals could work, study, and shop at home, and enjoy new forms of entertainment through the interaction of television, video recorders, computers, and laser technology. Building a data superhighway will speed the pace at which business and industry switch from military to domestic, peacetime research and development of existing and new products. Billions of dollars in government research

> Individuals could work, study, and shop at home, and enjoy new forms of entertainment through the interaction of television, video recorders, computers, and laser technology.

and development funds would be transferred from military to civilian commercial uses. Biotechnology, robotics, artificial intelligence, digital imaging, and data storage are some of the areas that will benefit. Another major benefit of the new information revolution is that it will give new hope and direction to America's high school and college students and graduates in finding skilled and high-paying jobs related to the new technology.

The information revolution is already on-line as a result of new inventions such as the early stages of digital and wireless telecommunications, fiber optics, and interactive audio and video technology. The goal is to enhance productivity by moving vast quantities of digital data seamlessly over high-capacity networks as sound, graphics, and video between universities, corporations, industrial research centers, health care facilities and, ultimately, every home and classroom.

In this series of four books on the new information revolution, author Walter Oleksy has interviewed technology specialists in business and industry, science and medicine, and entertainment, and has observed students and their teachers in electronic classrooms who are actively using much of the new technology. By joining them (so to speak) in these pages, you will learn more about the new technologies and the profound effects the developing electronic-data superhighway will have on your life.

Little over a decade ago, while tinkering in the California garage of one of their parents, two young men barely out of college invented and then marketed the Apple computer, which developed into a phenomenon and made them millionaires while bringing personal computers to the world. By learning about and using the new technology, you could be the next big player in one of the most exciting and potentially rewarding of futures—the electronic revolution that will speed us into the interactive multimedia age.

—Peter W. Frey
Professor of Psychology, Northwestern University
Senior Research Scientist, Pattern Recognition Systems, Inc.
Evanston, Illinois

Computers, fax machines, and other forms of information technology have become standard equipment in business offices. (Photo courtesy IBM)

# BUSINESS
## AND
## INDUSTRY

# Information Technology at Work

omputers, fax machines, telecommunications, and other
forms of information technology are changing the workplace, the worker, and the nature of many fields of work
more rapidly and broadly than perhaps anyone, even the
most future-predicting technocrats, imagined just a few
years ago. There are both good and bad sides to these changes, and
we will discuss them in this book, which deals with the uses of and
impacts of information technology on business and industry.

Millions of Americans use a computer at work, whether at a desk
in a traditional office setting or wherever else their work may be
located. In addition, nearly one in every three households now
contains a personal computer, and 21 million Americans work on a
computer at home at least one day a week. By means of computers
and/or fax machines, nearly four million Americans run home-based
businesses made possible by the technology, according to the Times
Mirror Center for the People and the Press in its 1994 report, "The
Role of Technology in American Life."

The survey's results were based on telephone interviews conducted under the direction of Princeton Survey Research Associates.

Closed-circuit television plays an important part in monitoring assembly-line production.
(Photo courtesy IBM)

A nationwide sample was taken of 3,667 adults 18 years of age or older, 400 young people 13 to 17 years of age, and an oversample of 207 adult modem users.

It should be noted that the figures quoted in this and other reports are transient in the fast-moving world of information technology. While these figures are significant today, in helping us gain some understanding of the rapid growth in the use of the technology in business and industry, their real importance lies in what they indicate for the future: there is a trend in the embrace of information technology in the workplace, and it is increasingly onward and upward.

Based on interviews with more than 4,000 people, the Times Mirror survey showed that 55 percent of those who work outside the home use a computer in the workplace. Computer use at work tends to be frequent: 43 percent of those interviewed use a computer at work every day or most days. Women are more likely than men to use a computer at work (62 percent to 49 percent). More than three-fourths of college-educated respondents (78 percent) use a computer at work, compared with only 18 percent among those who did not finish high school. Sixty-eight percent of college graduates earning $50,000 or more have personal computers at home, compared with 15 percent of nongraduates earning $30,000 or less.

The study reveals that even though the information superhighway is still in the early stages of development, computers and other forms of the communications technology have become an important part of the way business is conducted in the United States, both at the traditional workplace outside the home and in the growing number of home-based businesses. With a computer, fax machine, and telephone, employees and business owners can be in virtually instant contact with one another, or with those who buy, sell, supply, or market their products or services.

By connecting to the Internet, the global system of computer-modem-telephone networks, business can be conducted anywhere in the world by voice or printed word. For those who take advantage of the latest in telecommunicating technology, this can be done visually by videotape or even by real-life, real-time image and voice.

"While the building of an information superhighway may take years to complete," says the Times Mirror study's director, Andrew Kohut, "millions of Americans are already using the latest electronic technology to change the way they work, manage their homes and financial affairs, and entertain themselves."

> "While the building of an information superhighway may take years to complete, millions of Americans are already using the latest electronic technology to change the way they work, manage their homes and financial affairs, and entertain themselves."

The study found that Americans are much less intimidated or "afraid" of computers than many have assumed. "By a 65 to 30 percent margin, people said they like rather than dislike computers and technology," says Kohut. "They also believe computers and technology give people more rather than less control over their lives." The ratio was 42 percent favoring the technology compared with 17 percent who regard it apprehensively or unfavorably.

Interestingly enough, although the majority of American employees work and are comfortable with computers, many senior executives are "computer illiterate." A study conducted by Robert Half International concluded that "although technology is arguably one of the strongest driving forces in global competition, a survey of top executives on both sides of the Atlantic reveals that more than half of the executives in the United States (55 percent) and the United Kingdom (51 percent) are thought to be computer illiterate."

"Many top executives in both countries rely heavily on their management teams for work that requires computer use," says Max Messmer, chairman and chief executive officer of Robert Half International. "However, it won't be too long before this skill is a necessity. It already is for many senior executives, who use personal computers for everything from financial analysis to strategic planning to rapid communications."

Respondents to the survey, taken among more than 100 executives in each country, said that the main reasons for computer illiteracy among executives were that computer skills are considered a low priority and that many executives are intimidated by computers and discouraged about learning to use them. Resistance to change and lack of time were other reasons.

Meanwhile, virtually every business and industry has been affected by the information technology already in use—the computer, fax machine, modem, E-Mail ("electronic" or "voice" mail), and networking and telecommunicating. A fax (facsimile) machine is an electronic means of sending and receiving printed material. A modem is a computer accessory that translates computer data into tones transmitted over telephone lines, enabling users to send and receive text and graphics. E-Mail is a message sent electronically to and from computers via a computer network. Networking and telecommunicating are systems of interconnected computers, telephones, television transmitters or radios that enable users to communicate with one another electronically.

The technologies are speeding up the process of communicating in business and industry, enabling employees to operate more efficiently. To keep up with competition and control operating costs, existing and new technologies are being incorporated into virtually every business and industry, from airlines to telephone companies and from automakers to moviemakers.

The investment business is one example of an industry that is facing the future, utilizing information technology to meet the demands of doing business in today's computer age and into the twenty-first century. "This industry is in a technological revolution," says Peter F. Marcus, an analyst with the investment firm Paine Webber. So too are most if not all companies around the world today, forced by growing competition in the global marketplace to work more efficiently and economically. Existing products and services are being refined and new ones created to meet the demands of tomorrow's consumers.

Examples of the coming of the information revolution in business and industry are everywhere. Newspaper, book, and magazine publishers are rapidly converting to new technologies for the print media. The television and cable TV industries are being challenged by satellite technology that is expanding the reception capacity of television sets to as many as 500 stations beamed from around the world. Design experts at computer stations of the world's leading automobile manufacturers are working to develop safer and cleaner cars, while others are designing more efficient batteries to power tomorrow's electric cars. Architects are designing the homes and workplaces of the future. All are using computers in various ways and with a myriad of software programs that are tailored to help them solve problems in their individual fields.

"There is no doubt the Information Highway is here to stay," says Steven Levy, technology columnist for *Newsweek* magazine. "The problem is, we don't know where it's leading. We still haven't figured out how computers will affect the way we do business, conduct politics, protect our privacy, or produce jobs—or even how we think they *should*.

"There may still be plenty of stragglers who have yet to nuzzle up to computers, but there is no one unaffected by the explosion of computer technology. Everything from media to medicine, from data to dating, has been radically transformed by a tool invented barely 50 years ago. It's the Big Bang of our time—we might even call it the Bit Bang."

In the following chapters, you will see how computers and other forms of information technology are being used in a wide range of businesses and industries. The examples given are by no means the only uses or the only users, but taken together, they demonstrate how thoroughly information technology is transforming the workplace. At the same time, it becomes apparent from brief looks inside various businesses and industries that many jobs are being phased out and new ones are being introduced, requiring technological skills obtained only by additional education and familiarity with, if not love of, the technology.

# 2

# Technology at the Office

The office of the future? It's already here!

For Ronnie Fox, a New York City lawyer, his office is literally within arm's reach. He wears an "Office on an Arm"—a complete communications console designed to keep him in touch with his business wherever he is. Something like Dick Tracy's two-way wrist radio—a futuristic gadget dreamed up in the 1940s comic strip—the "Office on an Arm" contains a computer, a fax machine, a telephone, and a videophone. Built by British Telecom laboratories, it is worn between the elbow and the wrist.

"We used to think that we were on the leading edge of technology when we could import a chart into a word processor," says Todd Drombrowski, sales manager of the word-processing division of Lotus Development Corporation, a major producer of computer business spreadsheets, databases, and word processors. "Now I work in an office where you can put a movie of the CEO (chief executive officer) making a speech in a memo that gets broadcast to every division all across the world in real time. I keep my work calendar in Lotus Organize and then I link it to our AmiPro (word processor) and print out a daily, weekly, or monthly schedule with every appointment I have."

By turning data into linked objects, Drombrowski can set up budgets complete with animated graphics, and then see every element

Large-screen televisions, computers, modems, and telephone lines are basic ingredients of business teleconferencing. (Photo courtesy ISR Inc.)

of his budget change every time he changes a number. Pie charts and bar graphs can all be altered easily on his computer, greatly simplifying the amount of time, and the number of people, needed for revisions.

Through the use of his computer, modem, and telephone lines, Drombrowski can access the Internet, a worldwide network of computer communications networks. He can get data on virtually any subject and exchange information or ideas with others in his field of work or, for that matter, with anyone about anything.

By "videoconferencing," using desktop computers equipped with network video capabilities, Drombrowski also can meet verbally and visually with others in offices around the nation or the world without ever leaving his desk. The technology packs voice, video, and computer data on an ordinary phone line. Sitting at his computer, he can talk to the person whose picture is displayed in a window on his monitor, work on a file together with the person, and share a drawing board.

Many companies are discovering that videoconferencing not only saves travel time and money, because employees do not have to physically attend meetings outside their office, but helps companies make money, too. Most banks have mini-video cameras at their automated teller machines for security, but banks such as Huntington Bancshares of Columbus, Ohio, also use their cameras for two-way videoconferencing, staffing bank branches remotely, and selling investments day and night.

"Desktop videoconferencing is a very powerful tool. It combines the power of a personal computer with face-to-face meetings."

Computers run the show in corporate teleconferencing, allowing employees to communicate visually and aurally over distances. (Photo courtesy ISR Inc.)

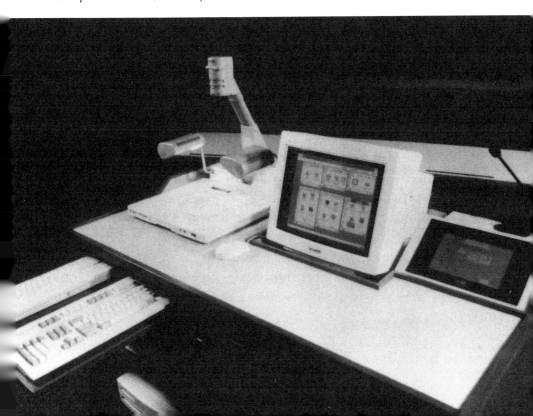

MEDITrust Pharmacy, a Canadian mail-order pharmaceutical firm, uses videoconferencing to create a "virtual pharmacy." By putting a video/phone/data kiosk in a convenience store and connecting it with a pharmacist at a remote site over telephone lines, the company can send medicines by mail.

Only 14,000 desktop video units had been installed worldwide by the end of 1993, but that number was expected to soar to 1.96 million by the end of 1998, according to a survey by Insight Research of Livingston, New Jersey.

"Desktop videoconferencing is a very powerful tool," says Frank Kavenik, vice president for development at NationsBanc, a holding company for multiple savings and loans based in Washington, D.C. "It combines the power of a personal computer with face-to-face meetings."

Kavenik and Drombrowski are typical of millions of Americans who use computers and other forms of information technology in their daily work. There is an almost mind-boggling array of machines, wires, and cables involved, designed to help people work more efficiently and thereby save companies money. Are jobs gained or lost by the technology? How has technology changed the workplace? Are employees more at ease or more stressed out using the technology? What technology is there, and how is it used? How did all this office high-tech come about?

In this chapter and those following we will attempt to answer these and other questions regarding technology in the workplace. For the sake of last things first, let's take a look at how technology in the workplace came about, not starting with what was perhaps the first office—a monastery cell in Germany in the Middle Ages in which a monk copied the Bible by quill and ink—but remaining closer to our own time.

After World War II, the typical business office was mainly equipped with a manual typewriter and a telephone. Within a few years, electric typewriters replaced manual machines, and copy machines (generically called Xerox machines) were added. Files and paperwork were stored on microfilm, to save room in file-cabinet storage.

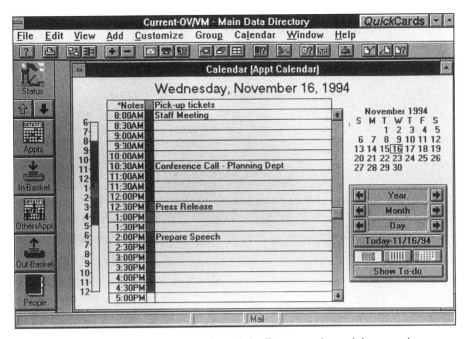

Appointment schedules accessed by computer software help office personnel meet daily time goals.
(Photo courtesy IBM)

The first electronic information-processing digital computer was built in 1946. But it wasn't until Remington Rand's introduction of the Universal Automatic Computer (UNIVAC) in 1951 that "mainframes"—huge, boxlike, multimillion-dollar computers—began to enter the workplace. The first customer was the U.S. Census Bureau. The giant computer featured mercury relay lines for memory and magnetic tape for input instead of the punched paper used in earlier computers.

UNIVAC remained the leader in the computer industry, despite the product's huge size and cost, until International Business Machines (IBM) introduced its 700 line of computers in 1955. Over the next five years, 2,000 computers came into use in government, university, business, and industry offices. In the late 1950s, transistors replaced electron tubes in computers, enabling them to be made somewhat smaller. The first automated computerized control system was installed at a Texaco refinery in 1959, and the following year it was used in banking. IBM computers were installed in thousands more offices and dominated the market until 1976, when Apple introduced the first small computers for personal use. Apple enjoyed widespread use in both offices and homes, generating competition that resulted in IBM's bringing out its own personal computer in 1981, giving new impetus to the growing revolution in office automation. Since then, computer makers have been constantly refining the technology to produce smaller machines that store more memory and do more things.

Computer technology has changed not only the way people work but also the way they interact at work. Various computer software programs enable office workers to better control information. For example, financial department employees use computerized business forms—software programs called spreadsheets. Architects create drafts of building plans on computers in simulated three-dimensional form. Automakers solve design and antipollution problems more easily and visually via computer. Aircraft controllers keep track of jet-plane traffic more accurately and safely through combinations of radar and computer.

The recent addition of CD-ROM (compact disc read-only-memory) drives to computers not only permits storage of the text and graphics contents of as many as 500 floppy discs on one CD-ROM disc but allows for interaction between user and computer. In the workplace, CD-ROM is used primarily for distribution of software and training materials. Its high storage capacity encourages businesses to use more images in documents. Desktop computers are playing an ever-growing role in the preparation of digital images for animation, video, publishing, and packaging. Kodak's PhotoCD process stores high-quality images on CD-ROM discs.

About four million CD-ROM players were sold in the United States in 1993, and the number nearly doubled the next year. By 1999, an estimated eight out of every ten computer users will have CD-ROM machines attached to their computers, while most new models have the feature built into their hard drives. Of about 8,000 CD-ROM titles that are available, fewer than 5 percent are for entertainment and education; these sell for from $30 to $100. Most titles are specialized business databases selling for $500 to $1,000.

A new class of CD-ROM titles is aimed at business professionals such as salespeople. Business 500, a CD-ROM from Allegro New Media, is a multimedia reference guide to America's top companies on one disc. It includes comprehensive and up-to-date information on more than 500 major U.S. companies. Sixty interactive videos show company products, and financial tables and graphs are available for easy reading, searching, and printing. Street Atlas U.S.A., from Delorme Mapping Company in Freeport, Maine, contains street maps of the entire United States on a single disc. It is a compact, easy-to-access sales tool that also can be customized for specific sales and marketing needs. Official Phonedisc U.S.A., from Digital Directory Assistance in Bethesda, Maryland, puts the nation's entire telephone white pages on one CD-ROM disc.

Computers and CD-ROM drives are not the only technology that is rapidly changing the workplace. By hooking up a modem to a computer, users can communicate around the nation or the world via telephone lines and satellites in space.

Telephone technology is moving just as rapidly as computer technology to upgrade and expand communications. Competitive pressures are pulling businesspeople away from their desks and onto the road in order to stay in touch with their clients and the marketplace. Technology connects them to the office. For example, a salesperson might need to work inventory levels, receive up-to-the-minute price quotes, run credit checks, and access office memos via E-Mail (electronic mail), which has become an indispensable tool of business, education, and government. E-Mail is created by typing a letter on one computer and sending it, by way of a modem, over telephone lines to another computer.

The most common way businesses connect to E-Mail is by subscribing to public on-line services such as Prodigy, Compuserve, and America Online. Letters are stored in an on-line service's central computer until the customer retrieves them. When both the writer and the reader are on the same computer network, E-Mail is delivered in just a few seconds.

E-Mail is also being used to update the time-honored tradition of office romance. Many users are communicating with potential romantic partners by sending courtship notes or poetry via computer and modem. "It's a wonderful combination of old-fashioned office courting and, at the same time, up-to-the-minute technology," says one female advocate of using cyberspace to find a future mate. On the other hand, complaints of sexual harassment and transmission of pornography over the Internet have been reported.

For the more businesslike task of keeping in communication with potential customers, salespeople have been using cellular telephones connected to laptop computers. Now, paging services and new wireless data services are challenging cellular phones. Today's paging services can send a full-page message to a PDA, a "personal digital assistant" device, such as the Apple Newton Message Pad, Casio Z-7000, and Motorola Envoy. PDAs are designed to accept advanced messaging or other wireless alternatives to cellular services.

Microsoft Corporation, a leader in computer software, introduced Microsoft at Work in 1993 to make it easier for computers, photocopiers, faxes, telephones, and other machines to talk to each other. With the new software, a simple push of a button turns what's on the computer screen into hundreds of copies. A fax machine can ship its information to the personal computers of dozens of people who need it all at the same time, and perhaps update a specific computer program. Many leading companies in copying and communications have pledged to use the new software, agreeing on common control standards that can more effectively link the world of paper documents with the digital world of electronic files.

Fax machines have vastly speeded up communications in business. Faxing notes, letters, reports, and even graphics is faster and often more dependable than using mail services because the time lapse between sender and receiver can be seconds instead of days. New faxing technology will allow users to fax from passenger seats on airplanes or in automobiles, and to read faxes on hotel-room television screens. Faxing is expected to be the next extension of the remote office beyond the telephone.

■ ■ ■

Fax machines send and receive documents and graphics faster than mail services do.
(Photo courtesy IBM)

Counting fax modems built into computers, there are about 11 million fax machines in offices and homes in the United States today. About two million fax machines are sold each year, according to BIS Strategic Decisions, a market-research firm in Norwell, Massachusetts, that specializes in the high-tech and telecommunications industries.

New office technology is not only transforming the way business is conducted but—for good or bad—changing the very concept of what an office is. Offices are no longer confined to buildings. Lightweight, battery-powered laptop and portable notebook computers account for nearly one in every six personal computers sold in the United States, according to Dataquest, Inc., market researchers in San Jose, California. They have enabled business work to be done practically anywhere, even on airliners. Sales representatives, field technicians, real estate brokers—anyone who ever works away from the office uses them.

"The office of the 1990s has four wheels, not four walls," says Perry Solomon, chief executive of High Technology Distributing in

Van Nuys, California. He now runs his business out of his high-tech equipped automobile, which has a computer, a telephone, even a fax machine that plugs into his cigarette lighter. His company puts out a monthly newsletter for 25,000 computer dealers, layouts of which are faxed to him in his car for approval. "It takes days out of the publication cycle," he asserts.

Taking workplace technology a giant step further, IBM began a planned nationwide downsizing of its company's office use by closing five branch offices in New Jersey in 1993. It gave up 400,000 square feet of conventional prime office space, with elevators, closed doors, and windows, and consolidated everything in a high-vaulted steel-walled industrial building in one location. At the new, consolidated branch office in Cranford, New Jersey, there are no enclosed offices, and no permanent desks for the 600 members of the sales and service force.

The move is typical of the changes being made in the workplace in general, brought about by technology coupled with global competition in the marketplace—changes that have enabled many businesses to reduce both space and staff. Of course, some of these "advances" are made at great social cost since, in many cases, people lose their jobs.

In many businesses and industries, the office is no longer a place where employees spend eight hours at a desk. Now they come for a specific task—to attend a meeting, to give a demonstration of the latest hardware for a client, or to pick up their mail. Gone are the private offices and even the high-walled cubicles employees treasured. With partitions between desks only about three feet high, everyone is visible all the time, even sitting down. No one puts up family pictures or gets too comfortable. Since there are only 220 shared sales and service desks, everyone can't be in the office at the same time anyway.

The company's general manager, Duke Mitchell, who also no longer has a private office, says, "I wanted people to know we're in a warehouse. No walls, no boundaries, no compartments." He told fellow workers, "You're here because of your competence, and there's no frills."

Workplace sociologists say IBM's consolidation of offices in New Jersey provides a glimpse into the office of the future. Kirk Johnson, writing in the *New York Times*, says IBM's approach is considered one of the most aggressive methods of tackling some of the dilemmas of the 1990s workplace: "How do you spin people out of the office to be mobile and competitive and closer to clients, and at the same time push them back in to work together in the group specialty networks that are so trendy? If you eliminate a person's private space, how do you maintain a connection with the workplace as a whole?"

"What we're starting to see is places that don't look like conventional offices," says Mike Brill, president of the Buffalo (New York) Organization for Social and Technological Innovation, which analyzes office work and office design.

As computer, telephone, recording, and copying technology continues to advance and become more interconnected, more

Computers are almost indispensable in keeping track of inventory. (Photo courtesy IBM)

changes may be expected in how employees work and what their workplace will look like. Chiat/Day, the advertising agency, and Ernst & Young, the accounting firm, both have begun "virtual offices," or hotel-style check-in offices in which traditional desks and offices have been eliminated.

The new IBM building's computers are specifically aimed at providing constant employee connection, with every personal computer linked to others. One room, called the "sandbox," is loaded with just about every competitor's products for employees and clients to try out. In another, designed for employee brainstorming sessions, people communicate by keyboard and anonymous messages from management are flashed on a large screen for all to see.

How do employees feel about the consolidation move and the loss of private offices? "As more and more individual work gets done elsewhere, in clients' offices or at home," says Duke Mitchell, "and as the office becomes accepted more and more as a place for group endeavors, patterns of work and style and thinking will change."

Workers under Mitchell's supervision say that the change has been less traumatic than they expected because the high-pressure, high-competition world of computer sales and service had already made most executives' and managers' offices only places for the occasional visit anyway. As one salesman put it, "In the old-style office, you had a picture or two. Well, now I keep the pictures at home."

When employees have time and are allowed to, they sometimes relieve office pressure by playing video games on their workstation computers. Some office managers even encourage the practice, believing that a little time-out for a computer game such as the shoot-'em-up game Doom can enhance productivity.

Government officials say there are also educational benefits to playing some computer games. Analysts at the Central Intelligence Agency in Washington, D.C., play a game that simulates social and political conflicts and their potential solutions in countries around the world. Employees at the U.S. Department of Justice play a game to sharpen their ethical skills; and Sim Health, a game that tackles health-care reform proposals, is popular on computers at the White House and in congressional offices.

Lighten up, say defenders of computer games in the workplace. Far from wasting time and shaving profits, playing games is actually useful. It teaches motor skills and acclimates employees to computers and the new technology; it relieves stress and fosters camaraderie among workers.

> "The traditional office is not quite an endangered species, but it's under definite rethinking."

Advances in computer and other information technology that have made work more portable and at the same time increased communication, combined with financial pressures in the increasingly competitive global marketplace, is forcing many businesses and industries to downsize in both office space and staff.

Kathleen Christensen, an environmental psychology professor who tracks office and workplace trends at the City University of New York Graduate Center, says, "The traditional office is not quite an endangered species, but it's under definite rethinking."

# 3

# Technology in the Home Office

Though two major surveys conflict as to exactly how many people work at home, both tend to indicate that the number is considerable, and growing. Nearly four million Americans run home businesses made possible by computers and other forms of information technology, according to a 1994 study by the Times Mirror Center for the People and the Press. In addition, almost one in every five Americans (18 percent) is self-employed at least part of the time. Nearly half of this group own home-based businesses, and at least half of these use computers and/or fax machines in their work at home.

In another study, LINK Resources Inc., a New York company that tracks uses of computers for computer makers, stock analysts, and other clients, reported that as of June 1993 some 24.3 million Americans were self-employed, working out of their homes full-time or part-time—many of them as consultants to companies where they once were full-time employees. It is estimated that many if not most of these self-employed people use computers in their work, at home, or in rented offices.

"Computers make it just a snap to take your job out of the office and into your home," says Erica Swerdlow, a public relations specialist in Deerfield, Illinois. Wanting to spend more time with her

Computers and telecommunications enable millions of people to work at home.

(Photo courtesy IBM)

preschool-age child, she resigned from her job as an account executive for a public relations firm in another suburb, set up a computer-driven home office in the basement of her home, and created EBS Public Relations. Her husband Brian quit his job in Chicago and became the new firm's business manager and bookkeeper, and they hired a full-time account executive to seek clients. To get the business on-line, a computer network consultant, called an "integrator," linked the home office's computers by using adapters from Norvell Inc.'s Lantastic software.

WordPerfect software and a laser printer allow Mrs. Swerdlow to create news releases, business proposals, and other documents that are complete with company logos and other professional features. A CD-ROM drive in her computer enables her to search databases for potential customers on the same kinds of discs that play soft music through her computer while she works.

Using a fax/modem with her computer, Mrs. Swerdlow sends out hundreds of releases for clients, and sales-contact management software lets her and her staff keep track of people they contact for billing purposes. Her husband keeps the books on special accounting software.

According to the Times Mirror study, one of the most significant social trends of recent years has been an increase in the number of people working at home—either in home-based businesses or as "telecommuters"—people who work at home at least one day a week and communicate with their workplace by computer and telephone. The percentage of the U.S. workforce working part- or full-time at home grew from 21 percent in 1988 to 33 percent in 1993, according to LINK Resources. Many people start a home business because they were laid off and are unable to find a new job of equal position or salary. Some start self-contained businesses, while others become freelance consultants for previous employers. A desktop or portable computer, together with a modem, a fax machine, and a telephone, provides them with the basic information and communication tools they need to do their job and the means to stay in touch with clients. Nearly half (49 percent) of about 4,000 people who took part in the Times Mirror survey and said they work at home part- or full-time own a home computer, and most of these use it in their jobs. Thirteen percent use a fax machine. Of those who run a business from their home, 40 percent use a computer and 20 percent a fax.

The survey suggests that not only do personal computers facilitate working at home but also that regular users are more likely to have jobs that allow them to work at home. In the sample, 27 percent of the respondents worked at home at least one day a week, but among regular computer users, 57 percent did so. Two-thirds (67 percent) of regular computer users said they use their computer to help them work at home.

In the Times Mirror survey, more than half of those who worked at home said they use computer modems to access computer bulletin boards. The same proportion of respondents said they subscribe to one or more of the commercial on-line information services such as Prodigy, Compuserve, or America Online. About a quarter of the respondents said they dial up often on the network to get financial information that they use in their home-based business.

Many computer software programs are available to help the self-employed set up home business offices. One such program is WordPerfect Office 4.0, which can service the communicating and networking needs of companies of any size on a global scale. It combines comprehensive calendaring, scheduling, and task management programs with electronic mail capabilities that automate the flow of work and information within and outside the home office to any distant source with whom the home worker wishes to be in contact.

> . . . one of the most significant social trends of recent years has been an increase in the number of people working at home, either in home-based businesses or as "telecommuters"—people who work at home at least one day a week and communicate with their regular workplace by computer and telephone.

Another comprehensive home-office computer system is Microsoft Office, which allows users to access any of Microsoft's business software so they can work together as a single system. This software includes Microsoft Word for word processing; Microsoft Excel for creating spreadsheets, charts, and graphs; Microsoft Access database for keeping track of clients' needs; and Microsoft Power-Point for creating effective business and marketing presentations.

Many people who work at home or run home businesses own not only a desktop computer but also any one of a variety of portable, battery-operated "power-book" computers that they can take with them on a train or plane, and work on in a hotel while waiting to attend a business meeting in a distant city. Top-of-the-line portable computers, such as the PowerBook Duo System from Apple Computer Inc., transform themselves into powerful desktop computers.

High-tech portable computers can work with printers, modems, and fax machines to put business travelers on-line as well. Whether these computer users work in a branch office, a client's office, or their own home office, portable computers make sure it is always "business as usual."

You don't have to be a computer whiz kid to run a home business with a computer. Art Bower of Beverly, Massachusetts, hardly knew how to use a computer when he started his own business in 1992. Today, as owner of Bower Associates, a manufacturer's representative for industrial-process heating products, he is literally a one-man computer office. He doesn't have a secretary or an accounting staff, just himself and his laptop computer.

"I was fifty-seven years old when I started my home business," says Bower. "It just goes to show that you're never too old to learn new tricks."

Bower needs to be constantly on-line with his customers because his sales territory covers most of New England and his products come from eight different countries.

"As a sales rep, I guess I can be called information intensive," says Bower. "Customer lists, sales histories, product availability, and commissions must all be tracked. Every piece of information I need is stored on my computer."

A word-processing program lets Bower jot down memos and compose letters. He uses a spreadsheet to track sales commissions. With a database, he keeps records of customer sales, prices quoted for products, purchasing histories, and contact information such as addresses and telephone numbers. The laptop computer he uses also features a modem for automatically dialing the telephone and storing frequently called numbers.

"I didn't invest in any specialized computer training to set up my home office," says Bower. "I simply read books, asked questions of technology suppliers, and fumbled around until I became familiar with the computer and it became an indispensable business partner. I still learn something new every day, and I'm always looking for ways the computer can make my work easier."

Home offices can be set up just about anywhere, but one of the most unusual locations is the basement laundry room of a home in Summit, New Jersey. David LaPier, an engineer, redefined the technology of telecommuting when he joined a test of a system called I.S.D.N. (integrated services digital network).

LaPier's employer, Bell Communications Research (Bellcore), the research consortium for the New England regional Bell telephone companies, had been trying for several years to create a market for I.S.D.N. With the network, customers can simultaneously send and receive voice and data, even video, over a single telephone line. Equipped with only a Macintosh SE computer and a specially outfitted telephone, LaPier became one of more than three dozen workers at Bellcore who participated in a six-month test of I.S.D.N.

All the bedrooms in the house were in use by LaPier, 36, and his wife Lucy and their three children, so the only place he could set up his home office was in the basement laundry room. His computer with modem and telephone answering machine sat on a desk. Mrs. LaPier, who works as an investment banker in Princeton, New Jersey, stayed at home part of the week, and the couple took turns caring for their five-year-old son and two daughters, one aged three and the youngest aged nine months.

Working at home, LaPier telecommunicated via speaker phone to Lynn Case, a coworker, in her office at Red Bank, an hour's drive

Owners of home-based businesses share information with others by computer and modem.
(Photo courtesy IBM)

away. The two could view a particular document on their computer screens at the same time, and could pass the cursor back and forth, as if one person were typing in a change, so the other saw the change immediately. They conducted simultaneous voice and data conversation through a single household telephone line.

Three days a week LaPier drove to his company's main office in Red Bank, 50 miles away. The other two days found him at home at his computer in the laundry room.

"Normally, you need more help at the office when you're not there five days a week," says LaPier. "But the I.S.D.N. phone line helped me to be a fuller member of the office staff, because I could work on the same computer files from either location." The file-sharing capability was based on I.S.D.N. "group ware" software called Aspect, by Group Technologies Inc. of Arlington, Virginia.

As of 1994, fewer than half of local telephone networks offered I.S.D.N., providing a basic component of home-office telecommunicating, but Bellcore is betting that the technology's time has come. John A. Meyerle, manager of the test project, says the main purpose of the trial was to give workers at home ready access to an employer's computing and communications networks. Since computer users like to coin high-tech words for being on-line, Bellcore has coined its own, calling telecommunicating "WAH," for "working at home."

"Before I.S.D.N., I 'sneaker-netted it,' carrying business-related floppy discs between home and office," admits LaPier. "But I was never certain I had the most up-to-date version of a file. The main thing I.S.D.N. let me do was get the latest version of files without any trouble. What more could a WAH-er need?"

Many companies are experimenting with home-and-office telecommunicating. In one such experiment, American Telephone and Telegraph Company (AT&T) offered a "Telecommuting Day" to employees, giving 123,000 of them nationwide a chance to take a day off, sort of. Instead of heading to the office on this day, nearly 19 percent of managers and other employees of the long-distance telephone company worked from home, using a personal computer, a fax, a modem, and a telephone. Sixty-nine percent said they were more productive at home.

The experiment was nothing new for Marvin Wamble, public relations director for AT&T in Washington, D.C., who had been working at home for about five months. His office is on the first floor of his two-story brick house in Fort Washington, Maryland, where he spends most of his day answering questions from the news media and writing press releases.

"I wear a golf shirt and walking shorts and sandals working at home," says Wamble, "so I save money on dry-cleaning suits, as well as gasoline for car travel and also lunch money by working at home. At lunchtime, I just dash to the kitchen and pop some leftovers into the microwave.

"The biggest advantage of working at home is I don't have to waste time or energy battling the brutal Washington traffic every morning. The only disadvantage is, sometimes, working at home, I think I work too much."

An AT&T employee in Chicago, Jean Eichenberger, an occupational health nurse, had commuted by train every morning for seven years from her home in suburban Glen Ellyn to the company's downtown Chicago office. She accepted the Telecommuting Day offer and stayed home to work in her basement office, finishing a report on her computer, processing disability claims, and making phone calls to recovering employees.

"I didn't watch daytime-television soap operas," says Eichenberger. "To avoid distractions, I didn't tell my three-year-old daughter I was downstairs working while the babysitter was with her. That made it a bit of a challenge to handle return phone calls. I doubt I could work from home full-time, but it's possible I could for a few days a week."

Workplace experts contend that telecommunicating increases productivity, reduces stress, and eliminates the time and effort spent commuting. Also, employees at home work in environments with better air quality than is found in most business offices. AT&T officials say their Telecommuting Day saved each employee who stayed home an hour of travel time and 2.2 gallons of gasoline. The environment was helped, too—it was spared 47 pounds of pollution per worker car.

Some of the newest generation of home-office hardware was used during AT&T's Telecommuting Day, such as:

- *Vistium*, a videoconferencing system that lets users in different locations work on the same document, even if they don't have the same word-processing or graphics software. It requires an I.S.D.N. digital phone connection.

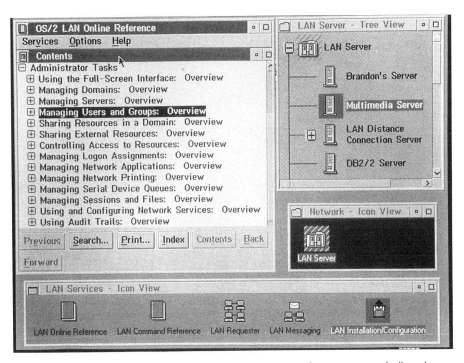

VoiceSpan modems allow computer users in distant locations to connect their computers and talk on the telephone over a single phone line. (Photo courtesy IBM)

- *Picasso,* a telephone that transmits high-resolution still images over rell images over regular phone lines in from 10 to 15 seconds. The images are captured from a video camera plugged into a telephone. A personal computer mouse also can be plugged in, so both sender and receiver can mark up a transmitted message.
- *VoiceSpan Modem,* which allows users to connect their computers and talk on the phone at the same time over a single phone line.

Nationally, small businesses employ 77 percent of telecommuters, while big businesses such as AT&T, American Express, and IBM have discovered they can save up to 25 percent on office-space costs by letting salespeople and agents work from home, according to the National Telecommuting and Telework Association. AT&T says it also benefits because most telecommuters need more telephones and make more phone calls to conduct business at home.

As the number of people who work at home at least one day a week increases, telecommuting technology will continue to be refined and improved. The easier it gets to work at home, and the more productive this becomes for employers, employees, and the self-employed, the more attractive and feasible working at home may become for many people.

For some, however, working at home may not be a blessing—or, at best, it may be a mixed blessing. Many factors must be considered, such as finding a suitable room for a home office, finding privacy if others are at home during the working hours, dealing with self-motivation without a boss or a supervisor present, and perhaps even loneliness.

For many whose homes are equipped with computer, modem, fax, and telephone, "Telecommuting Day" has already become "Telecommuting Every Day"—like it or not.

**4**

# Jobs and Infotech

S ome skeptics say that information technology (or infotech for short), which consists primarily of computing combined with telecommunications and networking, will eliminate many jobs because more work can be done faster by fewer people. They caution that high technology makes less-skilled people unemployable, just as tractors rendered horses unnecessary for pulling plows. Others, however, maintain that computers and other forms of information technology will mean more jobs for more people.

In many cases, infotech—which also includes expert systems, imaging, automation, robotics, sensing technologies, and mechatronics (microprocessors embedded in products, systems, and devices), and other interconnected technologies—is already reshaping the way workers do their jobs—in offices, factories, hospitals, classrooms, farms, and other workplaces.

"By the year 2010, infotech will effect many positive changes, making many jobs more challenging and rewarding, but it may also lead to job loss, depersonalization, or boredom," says Andy Hines, an associate of Coates & Jarratt, a policy research organization specializing in the future. He suggests that infotech will affect workers on two levels: "First, it will be an important tool that lets workers do

Computers, video and slide projectors, and other audiovisual equipment are essential in modern corporate offices and research centers. (Photo courtesy AMX Corporation)

The brains of AMX Corporation's business audiovisual system is its simplified Synergy remote-control system.

(Photo courtesy AMX Corporation)

more of their job through an intermediary, such as a personal computer or expert system. Second, infotech will change the nature of jobs because organizations will design jobs to take advantage of such capabilities. In speculating about future farmers, for example, we must consider that such technology will reshape farming."

How, specifically, will infotech change the way work is done in business and industry? This chapter and those following contain examples of the impact that information technology is already having in various workplaces. Briefly, here are some of the changes Andy Hines, writing in *The Futurist* in 1994, says are expected for some businesses and industries.

*Utilities* (gas, electric, water companies)—Workers in utility plants will use virtual reality (computer-simulated real-life workplace experiences) in overseeing automated operations. For example, a worker will manipulate an image of a part needing repair while tele-operated robots and high-tech equipment carry out the worker's commands. Workers still needed in the field to maintain transmission lines and respond to emergencies will use palmtop computers to obtain plant specifications on maintenance and repair, but they may need to spend only one or two days a week at field sites. Automation will eventually make jobs such as meter reading obsolete, as utility supercomputers will exchange data with traditional meters or a company's energy-management systems.

*Sales*—Salespeople will convert their cars or vans into mobile offices. The salespeople of 2010 will have little use for an office at headquarters. Instead, they will increasingly work on-the-road and at their customers' offices. Sales vehicles will be equipped with an array of electronic aids—portable cellular phones with voice recognition, digital fax machines, notebook computers, and even built-in videoconferencing capability. Technologies will make it possible to transmit orders directly from the customer's site to the factory.

Many routine meetings will be conducted by videoconferencing, freeing salespeople for in-person sales calls. Electronic or voice mail will handle less urgent communications. Imaging will become more important for selling. Customers will be able to see video or computer images of what they are buying, and try it out by using simulations. Salespeople will need strong information skills to supplement their "people" skills.

*Science*—Scientists will be able to work more easily in large groups, as infotech connects them with colleagues working on similar problems around the world. There will be much less "reinventing the wheel," as new knowledge is made available faster. Videoconferencing and groupware (software that enables workers in different locations to share the same information on their computer screens) will further enhance communication among scientists. Technologies will allow scientists to work on problems simultaneously or share the workload with colleagues in different or distant locations.

*Manufacturing*—Automation will continue to take a toll on jobs in manufacturing, but workers will need to be on hand to monitor and maintain robots and other equipment. In addition, there will be more opportunities in creative areas, such as designing, monitoring, and maintaining the automated systems, which will be the primary functions of factory workers or engineers.

*Farming*—Farmers will become farm managers and will primarily work indoors, where information will come to them as they oversee extensively automated "smart farms." Sensing technologies will feed data into computers that will analyze soil conditions, plant health, degree of ripeness of a fruit or vegetable, fertilizer mix, and moisture content. By 2010, farmers will perform market analysis, develop independent weather forecasts, and maximize growing conditions and output. They will enter instructions into computers that will then transmit the information to field equipment, which will do much of the work now done by farm laborers.

In all branches of business and industry, data visualization will be important for converting massive amounts of information into manageable form. Imaging technology will present data in attractive, easy-to-understand pictures, rather than tables and charts of numbers. While automation will become widely used in most businesses and industries, there will always be room for employees in any field of work to customize applications to suit their working style and needs.

"Computers make people more employable," says Benjamin Wright, editor of *Electronic Commerce Bulletin* of Dallas, Texas, who also believes there are many positive things about the changes infotech is already bringing to the workplace. "The computer revolution has fueled an enormous surge in jobs, and the reason is that the technology magnifies the productive power of people with

> "The computer revolution has fueled an enormous surge in jobs, and the reason is that the technology magnifies the productive power of people with limited abilities."

limited abilities. In the last fifteen years, millions of jobs have been created for non-professional employees who operate computers."

Electronic communications has also opened many new markets to people who have goods or services to sell—from basket weavers to musicians—regardless of their technical skills or level of education. Before fax machines became widely used, small businesses were largely limited to serving local markets, but now these companies can do more nationwide business by means of faster communication with distant potential customers. As computer networks become more popular, the same ability to be in close contact with customers will increase sales possibilities.

"Downsizing" has become a feared word among employees in recent years at companies big and small, as management has attempted to save money by reducing the workforce. At the same time, more companies are eliminating jobs in nontechnical fields. For example, Aetna Life & Casualty, a major insurance company, has eliminated about 8,000 jobs in the past three years as part of a companywide "reengineering" plan that includes putting more technology in the hands of front-line employees.

Another example of the way portable computers and telecommunications have cost many jobs is at Travelers, another leading insurance company. Salespeople used to have to perform 30 separate functions in order to evaluate whether a business customer's insurance premiums matched the risk involved in providing it with insurance protection. The process of recording the information with pen and paper at the prospective customer's workplace and then having it go through the company's data-processing center and eventually to a mainframe computer took as long as 40 days. With the use of laptop computers and modems, the process now takes only about one day. The speeded-up process allowed the company to eliminate 120 jobs, for an annual savings of about $6 million.

The worker elite of the future, for many businesses and industries, will be "techies"—the young men and women with education and experience in computer and other information technology. The trend reflects what Stephen R. Barley, a professor at Stanford University's school of engineering in Stanford, California, describes as the "technization" of American labor. Since 1950, the number of technical workers has increased nearly 300 percent—triple the growth rate for the workforce as a whole—to some 20 million. With one out of every four new jobs going to a technical worker, the Bureau of Labor Statistics forecasts that information technicians, already the largest broad occupational category in the U.S., will represent a fifth of total employment within the next decade.

Many companies are starting to make the mastery of a technical specialty a prerequisite for career advancement. At Union Pacific Corporation, for example, every new employee who aspires to a management position must first become a "data integrity analyst." Why? Because the railroad carries 13,000 shipments a day on 700 trains running on 19,000 miles of track. Coordinating that massive traffic flow poses a huge data-management challenge, one that requires a new approach to the rail business.

"We saw that the company's future growth would depend on the ability of our managers to be masters of technical data rather than overseers of the hourly workers," says Jim Damman, national customer services vice president.

Layoffs resulting from increased use of technology in the workplace also can mean job opportunities for those with the right new skills. While automation in manufacturing has cost tens of thousands of semiskilled industrial workers their jobs, new careers have opened up for factory technicians who know how to operate the new, computer-controlled production equipment.

"Employers who automate but take people out of the process are lobotomizing their factories (making them 'brain dead')," says Tom Blunt, a manufacturing consultant in Louisville, Kentucky. "A human is the cheapest, lightest, totally flexible, and reprogrammable machine money can buy."

Young people who train today for the jobs of tomorrow will be in great demand in all fields. "The key raw material in technology is people," says Nathan Myhrvold, head of research at Microsoft Corporation. "Recruiting high-caliber people is always a top emphasis here, and finding people of the right caliber is hard. If a company fails to attract top people, the future of technology at that company is limited."

From the smallest of start-up companies to the top 500 corporations in America, the strategies of high-tech talent scouts are much the same: Watch student prospects early and build durable relationships with them.

"We have a Ph.D. working for us now who was identified in high school," says Frank Johnson, manager of research and development employment and university relations for American Telephone & Telegraph Company's Bell Laboratories. "One of our current supervisors drew our attention twelve years ago as a promising physics student still in high school. He attended Purdue University's electrical engineering school on a Bell Labs scholarship and joined the company upon graduation. The company later sent him back to Purdue for a master's degree and he now helps oversee development of the company's new high-powered computer chips."

Many of the most employable young people today are recruited for top jobs because company personnel scouts maintain close ties with instructors in university computer and engineering departments. It is the same as professional basketball and football scouts keeping in touch with high school and college athletic coaches. Corporate personnel scouts say their constant contact with faculty members and former employees often results in advance, informal notice of an up-and-coming student.

"I get calls and visits, particularly from companies where we have alumni working," says Harry Lewis, a computer-science professor at Harvard University. "Some companies supplement their contacts by asking recently hired employees to review names of current students and point out exceptional candidates. Each generation recruits the next."

While many new jobs are available for those who can put their knowledge and expertise to good use in various businesses and industries, others are open in the information-technology industry itself, such as in companies producing interactive and multimedia hardware and software. Competition for available jobs, however, is strong, especially in smaller companies engaging in fields such as multimedia.

"Even though multimedia has arrived, it still doesn't have a lot of money behind it," says Debra Palm, managing director of the International Interactive Communications Society, based in Beaverton, Oregon. The organization's membership doubled in 1993 to 3,500, and about 300 new members now join each month.

Competition for jobs in multimedia is stiff, and those who land them tend to have a unique combination of talent and training. Some have Ph.D. degrees in physics and have taught at the college level; some have had movie or television script-writing experience. The varied backgrounds are needed in order to develop educational software on science and other technical subjects for the mass market.

Work-management specialists predict that infotech will continue to change the nature of jobs and the way workers do their work, affecting as much as 90 percent of the workforce by 2010. Most people will be primarily information workers who incidentally make rollerblades, sell sports clothes, oversee a factory assembly line, or grow corn. Their principal activities will be gathering, creating, manipulating, storing, and distributing information related to products, services, and customer needs.

"The infotech revolution is still in its infancy today," says Andy Hines. "But for workers, the old saying 'you ain't seen nothin' yet' is probably fair warning."

Louis Richman, writing on the opportunities for technology in the workplace for *Fortune* magazine, sees many benefits ahead for techies: "The new power of the technical workforce is liberating employees from the monotony of the industrial age. It's also providing companies with the know-how to alter their destiny—to make competitive leaps, to break into new markets. And it offers employees wider horizons and far more opportunity than any generation of workers has encountered before."

Both employers and educators agree that education will provide the foundation for tomorrow's employees to be successful in the information revolution. "Schools must use technology in order for students to learn," says Lee Droegemueller, Kansas's commissioner of education and a member of the Council of Chief State School Officers. "Technology connecting the school with the home and work will make learning relevant and useful. Learning will have no boundaries, as students can connect with others to access information, ideas, and experiences from within the community, across the state, and around the world."

Sandy Fitch, who teaches business education at Yarmouth High School in Yarmouth, Maine, applies this concept to her teaching. Two years ago, she had grown bored with her old teaching methods using textbooks and standardized tests.

"More important, I was concerned that my students weren't getting the hands-on training they'd need to compete in the workplace," says Fitch. "Then I plugged a Macintosh personal computer into my classroom teaching. I developed a three-month project in which each student was asked to complete eleven business-related activities, all on the Mac I brought to class."

The students started in right away with enthusiasm. They wrote resumés and assembled databases (information sources) of employees and salaries. They produced a company newsletter and even created a corporate profit and loss statement. When they finished, they were evaluated on their innovation and creativity, as well as on their ability to follow directions and write—all critical workplace skills.

"What a difference!" says Fitch. "Their work, and their evaluations, improved dramatically. They really got into the project, because it had meaning for them. Working on the computer gave them a chance to be more innovative. Now my students have the skills for an entry-level job anywhere in the country. They're computer literate and have strong enough communication skills so they'll feel comfortable in the workplace. They're prepared for practically any office-computer environment."

"Just about everything we take for granted about work today is likely to change," says Arthur B. Shostak, professor of sociology at Drexel University in Philadelphia. "What we have to look forward to is that the only jobs that will be good jobs in the twenty-first century will be ones that smart machines cannot yet perform."

Shostak predicts that workers will be competing with machines for jobs, that more work will be done at home, and that much of what we do will be spread over 24 hours, rather than concentrated in the traditional 9 a.m. to 5 p.m. workday. "The key thing employers will be looking for is human distinctiveness," says Shostak—"characteristics such as imagination, creativity, and novel thinking that people possess but smart machines do not. Machine intelligence is not yet playful enough. Humans are the masters of surprise, wit, and connection-making, which machines do only randomly and not well."

> "What we have to look forward to is that the only jobs that will be good jobs in the twenty-first century will be ones that smart machines cannot yet perform."

Some amazing jobs will be open for techies in the future, predicts Shostak, a member of the World Futurist Society, who obviously has a sense of humor: "There will be cyborg technicians who will work with human beings who have so many artificial body parts that they need a technician to keep things humming. Software talent agents will visit high schools and colleges to recruit people whose innate aptitude is for devising software. Holographic inspectors will supervise transmission of shimmering images of coworkers as part of the answer to the problem of isolation of telecommuters. And asteroid miners will work off moon stations to study the mineral wealth of asteroids. It will be a dangerous but lucrative job."

Whether or not these jobs ever need filling, it appears certain that techies in tomorrow's workforce will need computer and other

Computers and other information technology enable businesses to increase productivity.

(Photo courtesy IBM)

information-technology skills, not only to get a good job but to advance in it.

## Technology and Productivity

The information technology that is causing a revolution in the way work is being done in virtually every business and industry is being blamed for thousands of people losing their jobs. To these people, including many middle managers whose positions have been eliminated by technology, the "productivity revolution" is a threat, not a blessing. Yet history tells us that technological revolutions eventually create more jobs than they destroy. For every lower-level position eliminated by technology, new industries and job skills have been created.

"Over the past two hundred years, there's been no tendency toward rising unemployment because of people being kicked out of jobs by machines," says Joel Mokyr, an economic historian at Northwestern University in Evanston, Illinois. "It hasn't happened—not here in America, not in Europe, and not in Japan."

Technology has brought about increased productivity and is already spawning new job-creating industries in fields ranging from scientific research to education to entertainment. The reason is that technology allows products to be made more efficiently and thus holds down price increases, which results in greater sales. Increased economic activity translates into more jobs.

In the 1980s, U.S. businesses invested $1 trillion in information technology. For years, however, little payoff was seen from this investment. "Profits were flat, and productivity growth was stagnant," according to a 1994 *Business Week* special report on technology and the information revolution.

Signs of the "big payoff" from technology finally began appearing in 1993, with the economy coming out of recession and corporate profits improving. Productivity specialists give much of the credit for the upturn in business to corporations "reengineering" their workplaces—investing in information technology, thus enabling them to streamline their operations, from office management and factory production to marketing, advertising, and other aspects of business.

Just one example of how technology improves productivity can be seen at Fannie Mae, the nation's largest buyer of home mortgages. About three years ago, the company invested $10 million in new computers, to replace outdated mainframes that officials decided were hindering further business expansion.

Fannie Mae began reengineering itself, breaking down the old centralized departments that slowed work down. The departments were replaced by work teams that linked financial, marketing, and computer experts into a network of more than 2,000 personal computers and new software that make the machines accessible to workers with a minimum of training.

The $10 million investment in new technology paid for itself in less than a year. When interest rates plunged in 1992, the company was technologically able to handle $257 billion in new-home loans, nearly double its 1991 volume. It only had to add 100 more employees to a work force of nearly 3,000.

"If we had not used this technology," says Vice Chairman Franklin D. Raines, "our business would have collapsed." Instead, Fannie Mae's profits jumped 13 percent, to $1.6 billion.

In another example, when Aluminum Company of America, based in Addy, Washington, began to feed production data from its office computers back to workers on the factory floor, productivity increased by a dramatic 72 percent.

Similar productivity improvements are reported by owners of smaller businesses. In a 1994 survey by Opinion Research Corporation, 95 percent of owners of small businesses with fewer than 1,000 employees said that computer technology is "critical" and "important" to their company's survival. While some said they could not see a direct link between use of information technology and their profits, many others reported that the technology improves office and/or factory efficiency. This increases productivity which, in turn, results in more sales or increased savings, or both.

"Productivity gains come not because the technology is whiz-bang," says Gary W. Loveman, a Harvard Business School professor, "but because it supports breakthrough ideas in the business process." For Fannie Mae, changing the process meant doing more work with just a few more people. For dozens of other corporations, reengineering has meant being able to take on more work, even while downsizing. That, say business managers and economists, is the formula for a productivity explosion.

# High-Tech Job-Hunting

Computers, compact discs, modems, and fax machines are also important new aids in finding jobs.

The time-honored process of looking through newspaper help-wanted ads to find a job has gone on-line. The *New York Times*'s FasTrak is one example of how newspapers are joining the information revolution in the area of job searching. It offers a service by which job seekers can register their resumés with FasTrak's database.

First, you register with FasTrak by telephone; then you send your resumé to the service by fax machine. For a small fee, FasTrak delivers the resumé to as many prospective employers as you like. You can follow the process by looking for a FasTrak ad in the newspaper, then calling the FasTrak hot line phone number and, on your computer, punching in the code number for that ad. Your resumé is then sent to the employer via computer. The service costs $20 for six months of unlimited use. For more information, readers can call 1-800-340-JOBS.

Many producers of videotapes, computer floppy discs, and CD-ROM discs offer career-guidance software on subjects like how to find a job, how to succeed in business, how to be an effective people manager, and how to start and run your own business. Also offered are hundreds of tapes and discs on how to use computers and other technology in the workplace. You can play back the software at home or on a car audiocassette or CD player while you're driving to job interviews.

A set of ten videodiscs entitled Life Skills and Employability Skills provides examples of work situations specifically aimed at high school students in which they can interact with the software. The

Many computer-software programs help people job-hunt from home.
(Photo courtesy IBM)

series covers topics like Working with People, Dress and Grooming, and Career Decision-Making. A program called Success shows how eight students overcome personal obstacles to finding a good job, and Communications shows work situations in which correct and incorrect communication skills are used in job-searching. Job Interview and Resumé/Job Application discs help students experience the job-interview process. For more information, readers can call TT2D, Inc. in Ukiah, California, at 1-800-900-8009.

Many computer users go on-line to find a job by contacting others in their field of work over networking services such as America Online and Compuserve. One example is that of a former U.S. Navy pilot who lost his job because of military cutbacks. He went on-line to access a computer bulletin board for aviators and, through networking with other pilots, learned of work at a commercial airline.

With a computer and a modem, you can save a lot of time and energy in job-hunting and let technology do the pavement-pounding for you.

# Technology Aids the Handicapped

Technology is helping to reduce the 66 percent unemployment rate among the nation's disabled and handicapped, according to U.S. Department of Labor statistics. Many employees are finding that physically disabled people who may not be able to perform manual tasks are just as capable of working on an office computer as those who are not handicapped. When a disability affects a person's ability to work on a computer, technology can come into play to help overcome the handicap.

"With technology, we erased disability," says Donald J. Dalton, founder of Micro Overflow Corporation in Naperville, Illinois, who helps disabled people discover technology to help them find suitable jobs. "We make it transparent to productivity in the workplace."

Micro Overflow, which employs ten people, performs evaluations on disabled clients to learn their handicaps. It makes recommendations on computer hardware and software products that are available to clients to bolster their productivity despite their handicaps, and trains them in how to use the technology. The list of customers includes many major corporations that want to find employable people among the disabled. Other referrals come from the Illinois Department of Rehabilitation Services and the Veterans Administration.

"Micro Overflow strives to remove the 'dis' from disability," says Dalton, himself a quadriplegic, "and encourage each person's ability to its maximum in the least restrictive environment through use of modern technologies." Dalton uses a voice-activated computer to help manage his company. Speaking into a headset, he can activate the keyboard and type about 80 words per minute.

Information technology enables many handicapped people to work in traditional job settings outside the home.
(Photo courtesy IBM)

One of Dalton's clients, Patty Matteo, who is severely visually impaired, came to Dalton for help recently. After studying her situation, he recommended that special magnifying equipment and an enlarged computer monitor would enable her to work successfully. She was hired as director of development with the Deicke Center for Visual Rehabilitation in Wheaton, Illinois, which provided the special equipment she needed. Now she performs fund-raising, public relations, and desktop publishing duties for her employer.

"Prior to my using a computer, it was hard to find work," says Matteo. "The technology has made a big difference in terms of securing a job and maintaining it."

Some technologies that are helping the disabled in their work include:

■ ■ ■

- Voice-activated word-processing equipment for clients with motor-skills disabilities that prevent them from typing.
- Screen-review products that read information typed into a computer, allowing clients with visual impairments to proofread their work.
- Magnifying devices and oversize monitors for the visually impaired that enlarge characters, documents, books, magazines, pictures, graphics, and handwritten letters.
- Voice-recognition systems that allow physically disabled people to take notes by speaking instead of typing, and print-recognition devices that read typewritten documents aloud.

Dalton says that about 40 percent of his clients go on to form their own businesses, while the remainder work for employers. Some clients have started desktop-publishing businesses, while others are even more creative, such as the blind couple who use computer technology to run a home-based sports-broadcasting business. They listen to broadcasts of sporting events, then package the highlights and sell them to radio stations for rebroadcast. Computer technology helps them to store and retrieve information and perform administrative tasks.

Each year, hundreds of people with physical or learning disabilities are given help in finding and holding productive jobs by means of the multimedia and interactive computer programs Jean Campbell employs at the Choices Center she operates for the disabled in Port Chester, New York. "It's not a school," says Campbell, "it's a multimedia learning center to prepare the disabled for employment."

Campbell teaches people with disabilities how to design, produce, and market signs, posters, newsletters, and other graphics by using desktop-publishing computer software. The disabled work together with those who have no handicaps, learning how to perform various jobs in an atmosphere that duplicates a true design and production company. Recently, Campbell began working with local high schools on a project that enables special-education students to learn computer skills and experience a transition from school to the workplace.

Campbell's special interest in helping the handicapped came about because her brother was born severely disabled. "I promised myself that if ever something seemed to offer equal opportunities for the disabled, I'd seize it," says Campbell. While designing computer software for school use in 1991, she found that promise in interactive software: "The demand for it far outstrips the skilled labor pool. That's what I'm counting on ... filling the pool with talented, trained disabled people."

Thanks to computer and other information technology, and to people like Don Dalton and Jean Campbell who teach them how to use it, thousands of disabled and handicapped people are finding new jobs and discovering a new life.

# 5

# Advertising

S oftware that can turn a computer into a virtual television recording studio is helping advertising agencies to reduce their reliance on expensive middlemen in the creation of television commercials and save their clients a lot of money. A commercial production company may charge an ad-agency up to $1,000 an hour for its services. Ad agencies that can create television commercials themselves with in-house computers and video software can save so much, they may only need to bill a client $175 an hour while producing virtually the same commercial. The software, costing only several hundred dollars, contains graphics technology that many experts say is equal to the standard equipment used by production studios—equipment that costs hundreds of thousands of dollars.

Traditionally, ad-agency personnel would draw out an ad, shot by shot, on a storyboard (a printed rough draft of a commercial). Video would then be shot and a production house would make the commercial. The ad would then be shown to the client. If the client wanted changes, the expensive process would continue until the client was satisfied.

Although most final versions of commercials are still being produced at production houses, rough preliminary versions are now

Art software such as Adobe Photoshop provides instant graphics for advertising layouts.
(Photo courtesy Adobe Systems, Inc.)

being done by ad-agency creative staffs on in-office computers. Special software in desktop computers enables ad-agency people to create storyboards containing sound and motion. Video images can then be put into the computer and manipulated into a rough commercial. The images are then transferred to a videotape and shown to the client.

The ad-agency's creative staff can alter the rough commercial until the client is satisfied with the ad's message and content. Only then is the commercial sent to the production house for a final version. The end result is fewer costly visits to the production house and fewer reshootings of a commercial.

"You're not blowing your whole budget up front," says Sally C. Face, manager of computer systems at BBDO advertising agency in New York City.

Previously, video playback on a personal computer was often limited to half-speed and could only be displayed on a small part of the computer's screen. Now, more powerful computers and improved technology for digitizing, compressing, and decompressing video signals allows full-motion, full-screen playback and fancy special effects like morphing, in which one picture metamorphoses (evolves) into another. This is accomplished with software such as Adobe Premier, Adobe Photoshop, Elastic Reality, and Macromedia Director. Many ad agencies are investing tens of thousands of dollars to have in-house computer-video departments built and equipped with the new technology. The equipment still costs only a fraction of what the larger, heavier movie and video equipment in production studios cost.

The newest trend in making commercials with computers is installing systems for editing digitized video signals, which can cost less than $20,000. Gerald T. Monti, executive vice president of Common Sense Inc., a consulting firm in Seattle, Washington, predicts that within five years, digital video will be used in nearly every aspect of TV-ad production.

# Interactive Advertising

Another major advance of technology in advertising is the trend toward the use of interactive media to attract customers. Interactive television is the name for the combination of television, telephone, and computer services.

The selling potential of interactive media, which allows consumers to respond instantly to advertisements through their television sets and computers, has major advertisers "scurrying around looking for opportunities to experiment," says Irving A. Taylor, ad coordinator for Toyota Motor Sales. "There's a tremendous future for interactive advertising, only no one knows when the future starts."

How fast ad agencies get into the interactive commercial age depends on how

> "There's a tremendous future for interactive advertising, only no one knows when the future starts."

quickly full-fledged interactive networks become available on home television sets. Because they cost billions of dollars to build, the networks are only in the testing stage at present. When they finally come on-line, perhaps a few years from now, they will make it possible for viewers to see an ad on their TV screen and immediately place an order, via their TV remote or a phone call.

Some interactive networks will be wireless, so advertisers will be able to reach people outside their homes. Ads can be sent to handheld computers or to dashboard screens, which are starting to appear in some new automobiles.

The possibilities, which are many, say ad executives, include:

*The Virtual Peddler.* Through the wonders of computer simulations, a TV star such as Candice Bergen can appear on your television screen and talk about the newest power tools from Black & Decker, or about Sprint's latest calling rates. Then she will inform you that you have a dinner appointment at 7 p.m. and that there are six pieces of E-Mail waiting for you to read on your computer.

A celebrity's voice and face can also serve as your "electronic agent" in a system that browses through cyberspace, shopping and collecting information about products of interest to you.

> "Television as an advertising medium is going to be reinvented by the new technology."

*I Spy.* Interactive communications will create tremendous amounts of information about consumers that is potentially of "great help to advertisers," says Thomas Lopez, chairman of Mammoth Micro Productions, a subsidiary of the *Washington Post.* "The operator of your information highway will have the ability to monitor your every keystroke, giving him the knowledge to customize ad messages on your TV screen."

"Television as an advertising medium is going to be reinvented by the new technology," says Nob Alter, vice chairman of the Cabletelevision Advertising Bureau in New York City. "But I think we have the opportunity to improve it and make it more effective."

Advertising agencies such as Young & Rubicam in New York are establishing new departments to explore the implications of new technologies such as interactive television, which can offer new ways to increase agency revenues and corporate profits.

"The new technologies will open up new markets to advertising we did not know were there before," says Mike Samet, executive vice president at Young & Rubicam.

# 6

# The Aircraft Industry

omputers, by modifying several processes in both engineering and operations, played a major role in the design and manufacture of the world's newest and largest jumbo jet in 1994—the Boeing 777. United Airlines put the high-tech jet into service late that spring.

In Boeing Commercial Airplane Group's engineering department in Seattle, Washington, traditional drafting boards became a design tool of the past as the 777 emerged as the first airplane to be 100 percent digitally designed and "preassembled" on computer screens. In Operations, the pencil-and-paper tracking system formerly used to log an airplane's assembly status was replaced by a more efficient computer system.

In designing the plane, the change was even more far-reaching than a simple move from two-dimensional to three-dimensional computer images. Boeing officials say computer technology is having a significant impact on the entire process of designing and building airplanes—resulting in improved quality, reduced costs, fewer changes and errors, and less work needing to be done over again. Typically, change, error, and rework are the highest cost factors for any manufacturing endeavor, but they run into astronomical figures in jet-plane design and construction.

56

Design/build teams used a three-dimensional computer system to design and preassemble the new Boeing 777 twinjet plane. (Photo courtesy The Boeing Company)

Boeing first began using CATIA (computer-aided, three-dimensional interactive application) in 1987 to design some of the parts for an earlier plane, the 747-400. It increased its CATIA experience a few years later with specially programmed three-dimensional digital computer software to meet unique aircraft requirements. In 1990, Boeing began using about 1,700 CATIA workstations in the initial design of the new 777 twinjet. These are supported by four connected IBM mainframe computers, the largest such installation of its kind in the world. The mainframe cluster is also linked to mainframes and workstation installations in Japan; in

> The ability to preassemble parts electronically on the computer screen allows engineers to find, and easily correct, misalignments and other fit or interference problems.

Wichita, Kansas; in Philadelphia; and in other locations. At the peak of the design process, more than 2,200 CATIA workstations were used, attached to an eight-mainframe computing cluster.

CATIA is a CAD/CAM (computer-aided design/computer-aided manufacturing) software system that enables engineers to design parts for jet planes as three-dimensional, solid images and then simulate the assembly of those parts on the computer. The ability to preassemble parts electronically on the computer screen allows engineers to find, and easily correct, misalignments and other fit or interference problems. It also eliminates the need to build a costly full-scale mock-up of a plane.

In the past, analysts and engineers who worked on an airplane's design worked with two-dimensional drawings and took turns adding elements to the design. CATIA's interactive capabilities allow engineers to work on various aspects of the design at the same time. Employees share knowledge and identify problems before tools or parts are even built. At the peak of the design process for the 777, 238 teams of employees from diverse disciplines worked on the plane.

In addition to designing the airplane with computers, 777 employees use computers to make the manufacturing process run more smoothly. A new system called Assembly & Installation Shop Floor Control was designed to make assembly-job information readily available to all employees.

"One of the principal goals of the 777 program," says a Boeing spokesman, "is to demonstrate an improved process for designing and building airplanes—a process that improves the quality of the end product and dramatically reduces design changes and errors, and the resulting rework. Whether in designing or building the airplane, the use of computing technology is playing a significant role in helping Boeing employees reach their goals of delivering service-ready airplanes on schedule and providing better value to customers."

# Interactive—Up, Up, and Away!

Another example of computer technology in the aircraft industry is the introduction of "interactive arcades" that passengers can play with during flights, taking the place of the old-fashioned in-flight magazine.

On a Virgin Atlantic Airways flight between Hong Kong and London, for example, an auction house executive played half a round of computer golf. Then he listened to a symphony on CD and watched a new movie.

Like many other air carriers around the world, Virgin Atlantic offers passengers multimedia computer entertainment to make the flights seem shorter and more pleasant. Planes are equipped with interactive computer screens that, for a fee, allow passengers to select their own movies and compact discs, book hotel rooms, and order merchandise. By some estimates, the interactive services could earn a million dollars or more each year for the average airline.

Virgin Atlantic, which in 1994 became the first airline to get a working interactive computer system in the air, says nine out of every ten passengers use and like it. On the other hand, after a short trial with interactive video for passengers, Northwest Airlines discontinued its use because of complaints from flight attendants that they spent too much time dealing with passengers whose equipment malfunctioned.

Some airlines ban passengers from using compact disc players or laptop computers in-flight, or at least during takeoffs and landings. They cite safety dangers—such electronic equipment may interfere with pilots' navigation or communications systems. Nonetheless, British Airlines and United Air Lines phased in passenger interactive computer systems on transatlantic routes in 1995.

The systems look like the offspring of a laptop computer and a portable telephone. A small flat screen is mounted either in the back of the seat or on the armrest. The keyboard, which doubles as a mobile phone, comes with headphones. Along with a choice of about a dozen new movies and travel films, the systems offer on-screen shopping, the ability to arrange for car rental, and language instruction in Japanese, German, Spanish, and French. Video games range from Nintendo's Tetris to interactive chess, enabling a passenger in seat 2C to play a game with someone in seat 34A.

"You think most passengers are serious businesspeople," says Steve Ridgeway, director of marketing at Virgin Airways. "But there they all are, playing Nintendo."

Besides interactive fun and games in the sky, information technology also enables airplane passengers using "airphones" to carry on telephone business anywhere in the world as they fly to their next meeting.

> "We see no technical reason why over the next several years the satellite system will not become the only navigation system. This is certainly the most significant aviation advance within our lifetime."

Reservations are already computer-generated in airline and travel agency offices, but a step further is an electronic flight-booking and travel agent. With the use of a wireless handheld computer, customers can enter their preferred travel date and time, airline, and credit card number. The computer's Telescript software sends the booking request, via radio waves, to a computer network connected to the airline's reservation and ticketing system.

Commercial airlines may soon use a satellite-based navigation system for landing in bad weather. The Global Positioning System will be used by more than 1,000 American airports in an initial experiment to aid in landing under adverse weather conditions. "We see no technical reason why over the next several years the satellite system will not become the only navigation system," says David R. Hinson of the Federal Aviation Administration. "This is certainly the most significant aviation advance within our lifetime."

With commercial air traffic expected to double in the decade ahead, FAA engineers are designing a highly automated $32 billion computer-control system to reduce delays and enhance safety.

But while safety may be enhanced with new technology, many pilots wish they could go back to the good old days, before flying on automatic pilot, when they had the cockpit, if not the sky, more to themselves. "Now pilots are really more of a computer systems manager than anything else," laments Richard Obermeyer, a 13-year pilot for USAir, as automation shifts pilots' roles.

"Now, pilots don't even decide how fast to fly," says Dave Greenberg, a 30-year pilot. "Their flight computer does. A cockpit isn't even called a cockpit anymore. It's called a flight deck."

The good old days of flying may be gone forever for some pilots, but computer and other information technology is making the future brighter for many aspects of flying. Airline-industry analysts predict that more planes will be designed, built, equipped, and flown with the new technology.

# 7

# Architecture

W hen terrorists set off an explosion in the basement of the World Trade Center in New York City in 1993, extensive damage was caused to six underground levels of the skyscraper's twin towers. Some of the buildings' vital operating systems, such as heating, air-conditioning, communications, and police and security had also been badly damaged. Architects and engineers used computers to help them determine the extent of damage and create plans for rebuilding. Those specialists directed a small army of electricians, carpenters, plumbers, and laborers who repaired the building complex.

The rebuilding process largely centered on an enormous computer-generated repair program called the "critical path method." Several times a day, a personal computer created a fresh map, which city managers and contractors used not only to figure out the daily procedure for repair work, but what to do next, where to expect delays or other problems, and where to concentrate their efforts.

Displaced from his office in the Trade Center by the bombing, Robert DiCiara, assistant director of the World Trade department of the Port Authority of New York and New Jersey, worked from a corner of a former restaurant at the Trade Center. He could get along without his office but not without his organizing and management system, which was run by one desktop computer and six laptops. The computers helped him direct thousands, if not millions, of tasks—from bracing girders to installing emergency lighting—that affect one another in many critical ways, many of them interdependent.

"The human mind isn't very good at combining lots of uncertainties," says Robert N. Harvey, manager of the Port Authority's Office of Capital Programs. "We can't handle much more than 'Will

Computer graphics and CD-ROM software help architects design and construct buildings and landscapes. (Photo courtesy IBM)

> "Teenagers' personal home environments should be designed to be responsive, adaptive, and interactive."

it rain on the job tomorrow?'" Computers helped architects and engineers foresee and handle multiple problems at once.

The nerve center of repairs was DiCiara's operation, and the main tool was a computer program called Primavera, running on a clone of an IBM personal computer. The computer system included a plotter (a kind of computer printer that produces poster-size charts) and some fax machines and modems for trading data with consultants around the city and the country.

Thanks to computers, most of the monumental repair work was accomplished within a month, and workers and tenants were able to return to their offices.

For less-ambitious projects, there are many computer and CD-ROM software programs that help architects with the design and construction of commercial and residential buildings and with landscaping. Over the past 15 years, architects have been replacing their drafting tables with computers and working in the world of CAD (computer-aided design) software programs. Some programs, such as My House, Design & Build Your Deck, and Visio Home, offer even nonprofessionals the means to design everything from new kitchens to entire houses to furniture layouts for every room. Many of the software packages come with three-dimensional capability, so that with the click of a mouse, you can see your design from a variety of angles. Prices range from about $15 to $150.

David Pesanelli, an architect in Rockville, Maryland, uses a computer to help him design futuristic homes. One of his most exciting projects is designing the teenager's bedroom of tomorrow.

"Teenagers' personal home environments should be designed to be responsive, adaptive, and interactive," says Pesanelli. "Their room could be constructed as a matrix, or platform, within which spaces and components could be easily arranged each day, to nurture their creativity, imagination, curiosity, and keen observation."

In an interactive matrix room, Pesanelli says teens could adapt their "often rigid home environments" to suit their sizes, games, and imaginations. He envisions a room with a plastic pod containing a computer and video screens to provide access not only to entertainment and games but also to information needed for school assignments or imagery for playful experimentation.

Pesanelli uses an Aldus architectural drawing program for designing and problem-solving. "If I didn't use a computer, it would be a lot more work and require more employees. For eighteen years, about a quarter of my work was doing designs for feasibility and cost-cutting and prototype studies. I had a staff of helpers. Now, with computer software, I can easily do it myself. The computer is an extremely helpful tool in helping me put together all the designing and planning for a project."

Computers and their graphics capabilities, enhanced by three-dimensional visualization and multimedia features, will make it possible for architects to solve residential, commercial, and industrial design problems that are already anticipated for building in the next century.

# 8

# Art and Design

omputer graphics have many applications in business and industry in the areas of art and design.

National Aeronautics and Space Administration designers are at work creating three-dimensional designs for replacement parts to be used in future space stations. Designs for parts that exist only as data in a computer will someday be transmitted anywhere, even into outer space, where a machine will create them from raw materials.

Baxter Laboratories in suburban Chicago, a maker of hospital supplies, uses computer-generated rapid prototyping to produce models of new products such as intravenous solution equipment and needle-less connectors. Rapid prototyping began in the late 1980s with a process that uses a laser beam to form a hardened object out of a bath of molten plastic. The process begins with a computer-aided design terminal manipulating data about the object. In effect, the laser electronically cuts the object into hundreds of horizontal slices until an object is built from multiple slices.

Supercomputer graphics are enabling engineers to redesign the traditional parachute. The technology is giving scientists clues as to how to tackle the problem of exactly how air and fabric interact to make parachutes work.

Conservation artists at the Museum of Modern Art in New York City are using computer technology together with stereo microscopes to remove discolored varnish from masterpieces and restore the original beauty of many famous paintings. Another technique, infrared reflectography, sends infrared light through the surface of a painting, sometimes revealing a painter's previous work under a finished piece.

> "Computers have gradually acquired the ability to take some of the drudgery out of video production."

One of the most widespread uses of computer graphics in business and industry is their application to presentations. For

Video Toaster computer software replaces huge and more expensive equipment necessary for video production. (Photo courtesy NewTek)

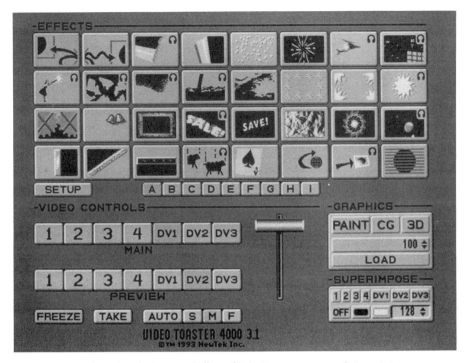

Computer-generated visuals and other special effects of Video Toaster are accessed via an Amiga computer. (Photo courtesy NewTek)

example, digital-desktop computer video enables the art departments of advertising agencies to create multimedia and interactive presentations for current and prospective clients.

NewTek's Video Toaster is one important tool of desktop videography in the creation of presentations. "Computers have gradually acquired the ability to take some of the drudgery out of video production," says Rick Lehtinen, an Arizona-based specialist in desktop video, multimedia, and video production.

What can computers do for videographers? Tasks range from scripting and storyboarding, on to editing the video footage, adding titles, graphics, and animation, and finally to distributing the finished video.

The Video Toaster, used exclusively with an Amiga computer, is revolutionizing video production for presentations and other graphics applications. It is an inexpensive, easy-to-use computerized video-editing system. The Toaster shrinks a roomful of expensive professional video equipment into a circuit board that fits into a Commodore Amiga computer. It is essentially another computer that manipulates images from any video source—a camcorder, a video recorder, or a television set. It acts as a seven-channel production switcher, special-effects generator, color-processing engine, character generator, frame grabber, and 3-D graphics-animation program all rolled into one. The personal computer is then transformed into a desktop video production studio. With the Video Toaster, art directors can create television-broadcast quality video for a fraction of the cost of video studio equipmment.

> What can computers do for videographers? Tasks range from scripting and storyboarding, on to editing the video footage, adding titles, graphics, and animation, and finally to distributing the finished video.

Four other leading presentation software programs used by the creative staffs of leading advertising agencies are Ca-Cricket Presents III 1.0, Symantec's More 3.1, Microsoft Power Point 3.0, and Aldus's Persuasion 3.0. They lead the field in organizing 35mm color slides, text, and graphics, creating charts, and giving on-screen presentations.

For example, David Anderson, owner of a consulting firm in New York City, uses his computer to tailor a presentation designed to expand his business of customizing and installing computer systems for both small and large businesses. He creates an audiovisual presentation with slides or video movies that he can use when meeting with prospective clients and when publicizing his business before organizations and at business expositions. His screen shows, because they are run from the computer, can incorporate graphics, animation, sound, and video effects. Not only can he apply transition effects that pan, scroll, or zoom to the next image; he can add music and sound effects to play as the images are shown.

> With the Video Toaster, art directors can create television-broadcast quality video for a fraction of the cost of video studio equipment.

Multimedia can be used to further enhance presentations. For example, instead of using a static bar graph to depict the returns of productivity that a potential client might expect to see, an on-screen presentation can show the bars actually growing on the chart. Other techniques are using an animated arrow to depict an upward trend, or playing a trumpet sound to herald increased profitability. Sound capabilities are created by adding a sound card and speakers to a computer, to record and play everything from music to voice-overs to sound effects.

Computer-generated video graphics are expected to play an increasingly important role in business and industry. At the same time, refinements of the Video Toaster and competing systems will take presentation technology into exciting new directions.

# 9

# Automobiles

S elf-navigating cars and "smart highways" that will take you to your destination without the need to put a foot to the gas pedal or a hand to the steering wheel are just a few of the computer-driven advances ahead for motorists and the automobile industry. Others are already here.

Sony Mobile Electronics and Etak, Inc. are offering an option that, through the use of a network of satellites, lets you navigate your auto by computer. It's a small computer with a built-in CD-ROM drive, designed especially for tourists, traveling salespeople, and delivery people, using the Pentagon's Global Positioning Satellite System and a detailed computerized road map. The map, which includes street names, shows up on a five-inch color computer screen attached to the dashboard.

Push a button and small knife-and-fork symbols appear to show you where to find nearby restaurants, with descriptions and ratings from a Fodor's travel guide.

> Push a button and small knife-and-fork symbols appear to show you where to find nearby restaurants, with descriptions and ratings from a Fodor's travel guide.

Parks, shops, museums, and other attractions are also included. The data is stored on two compact discs.

A slightly simpler version, City Streets, produced by Road Scholar Software of Houston, Texas, can be used with laptop computers. It covers street directions for 170 American cities and 80 more in Europe.

Similarly, Oldsmobile's Eighty Eight LSS automobile offers a $2,000 option called the Navigation/Information System. A small antenna in the car picks up signals from Pentagon satellites, and a small computer in the trunk makes calculations to determine the car's location as it travels the highways. A gyroscope and the odometer also feed information to the computer. The computer knows the names of streets, and it also knows which ones are one-way.

Information appears on a liquid-crystal display screen measuring four inches diagonally, attached to the center of the dashboard on an arm similar to one that supports a rearview mirror. But the

A dashboard-mounted minicomputer screen displays road maps for easy navigation in a car.
(Photo courtesy ETAK, Inc.)

Computers help engineers design new automobiles and parts for them. (Photo courtesy IBM)

system is still not perfect—until modifications are made, it can't warn you against an illegal U-turn.

Computers are also helping to build new automobiles and auto parts faster, more accurately, and less expensively. For example, they enable workers at the Ford Motor Company's electronic components plant in Lansdale, Pennsylvania, to produce 124,000 engine controllers, antilock brake sensors, and speed-control units a day. Since each product has 400 to 500 parts, managers have to keep track of more than five million individual pieces daily. Computers help them do that.

"The plant was designed with a high level of flexible automation and extensive computer controls," says Dudley C. Wass, the plant's manager.

Making use of bar-code technology to label and track virtually every circuit board, and relying heavily on computerized equipment that can be reprogrammed speedily, managers can trim inventories and introduce product changes rapidly.

"Our model is the cheetah," Wass says. "We want to be able to stop on a dime, direct all our energy toward a goal, turn quickly, and accelerate rapidly. Computers help us do that in designing and building electronic auto components."

Wass says he regards computer technology as information. It allows him to more efficiently access information to make the complicated, sensitive electronic parts the new cars need.

"Competition is fierce," says Wass. "It's a matter of being a time-based competitor. To do that, you need information to help you. Information gets to be a key resource. Computers give me the information I need."

Another avenue of progress in the automobile industry made possible by computer technology is the effort to design and build an efficient, economical electric vehicle. Computer-literate college students take part each year in this pursuit by entering the Hybrid Electric Vehicle Challenge, in which students from 40 U.S. and

Computers and other audiovisual technology are used by teams of student engineers at electric-car competitions. (Photo courtesy Argonne National Laboratory)

Canadian universities and colleges compete for the honor of designing and building the best-performing car powered by either batteries or internal-combustion engines.

At road trials in 1994 at Argonne National Laboratory near Darien, Illinois, student teams from three schools competed—the University of Illinois at Urbana-Champaign, the University of Wisconsin-Madison, and Jordan College Energy Institute near Grand Rapids, Michigan. While one student sits at the wheel and drives the car, another sits in the passenger seat and operates a computer that analyzes the car's every performance requirement.

On his team, Philip Guziec, 24, a University of Illinois mechanical-engineering graduate student, was in charge of the internal-combustion engine and emissions on his school's entry, "The Chief," named for the school's mascot, Chief Illiniwek. "What appeals to me about this is that it's not some pie-in-the-sky environmentally altruistic car," he said. "It can go as fast as 90 miles an hour and look virtually the same as a Ford Escort station wagon. But this couldn't be done without a computer figuring out precisely how efficient the electric battery is."

At electric-car competitions, student mechanics with grease-covered hands are almost as likely to pick up a pocket calculator as a socket wrench. A "tune-up" means plugging a laptop computer into the car to change the motor-control software.

James Worden, 26, of Wilmington, Massachusetts, began tinkering with computers and electric-car batteries while still in high school. Today he is co-founder of Solectria, one of the nation's leading independent designers and developers of electric-vehicle batteries. Shortly after graduating from the Massachusetts Institute of Technology in 1989, he founded the company with Anita Rajan, then an undergraduate and now president of the firm. A table in the lobby of the company's headquarters is jammed with trophies for endurance and speed won by batteries Worden and his team of engineers have designed—batteries that have helped them win many national electric-vehicle competitions.

"Computers have played a major role in helping us design and build the batteries for our electric cars," says Worden. "Improved battery design will be the key to increased power of electric cars, lower prices for them, and their general acceptance by the public."

"Advances in computer electronics are making electric cars more plausible, and energy-efficient, in a competitive world," says Thomas P. Newenhouse of Motorola, one of the largest producers of computer processors for cars.

Computers have clocked Worden and his engineers achieving speeds of up to 70 miles an hour and acceleration of from zero to 30 mph in seven seconds in their electric battery-powered pickup truck. These are major steps toward making electric vehicles a reality of the future. The technology also has important applications for cellular phones, miniature vacuum cleaners, and anything else that runs on rechargeable batteries.

# 10

# Banking

M any banks spent millions of dollars a decade or so ago to develop and offer services to customers with home computers, but not many people were interested in taking advantage of them back then. Now, with the number of home computers in the U.S. estimated at 30 million and growing, customers are increasingly at ease checking their bank balances, moving money between savings and checking accounts, paying bills, and opening new accounts using personal computers and new computerized telephones.

Today, many more banks are relying on information technology to give their customers the best service. This is based on a belief that as the younger generation that grew up on computers and Nintendo-type video games reaches maturity, most banking will eventually be done electronically rather than face-to-face between customers and bank representatives.

Several hundred thousand households in the nation now do a substantial amount of their banking and money management electronically from home via computer and telephone. For instance, Microsoft Money allows Chase Manhattan bank customers to print out their own checks on their computer printers and also make direct electronic payments. Quicken, a leading home-banking software

More people are doing their banking by computer and telephone, either in banks or from home computers and modems. (Photo courtesy IBM)

program, turns a home computer into a personal banking system for personal or business financial record keeping.

Some banks have already started closing neighborhood branches and replacing them with computer-telephone service centers similar to automated banking machines. Taking a lead in this trend is Huntington Bancshares, based in Columbus, Ohio, which operates 350 branches. It unveiled the nation's first interactive video-banking machine in 1994. The bank's plan is to close as many as 40 percent of its traditional branch banks in the area over a three-year period, leaving automated teller machines and specialized video-telephone devices in their place. Similarly, Chemical Bank closed 50 of its 320 branches in the metropolitan New York area, since 40 percent of its transactions are now handled through computer-telephone connections.

Other banks, such as the U.S. Bank Corporation in Portland, Oregon, are entering new electronic territory with fully automated offices rather than spend $1 million or so to open a traditional branch. During the next ten years, more than 40 percent of the nation's 100,000 bank branches will probably close, according to Joel Friedman, of Andersen Consulting. "Closer to 50,000 branches should provide adequate coverage and dramatically increase the earnings of the financial services industry," he predicted. Computers and telecommunications make these changes in the banking industry possible.

"Huntington has a boldness that sets it apart from other banks when it comes to thinking about what tomorrow's model of banking will look like," says Friedman. The bank has invested more than $25 million in developing a sophisticated array of electronic-banking services to replace face-to-face banking. These include a 24-hour telephone service with bank staff, and an automated telephone service for checking balances and paying bills that responds to recorded spoken instructions. Also available are two-way video telephones so customers can see the banker who is helping them open an account at an unmanned branch. Computers record and store all the banking transactions. The bank is also developing a

> "Customers increasingly want to do banking whenever and wherever they are." Telecommunications and computers help to provide these services.

telephone to rent to its customers for about $20 a month that has a computer screen displaying account information.

Huntington's biggest success so far is its call-in telephone service with automated teller machines and specialized devices allowing customers, at any hour, to apply for a loan and have it approved in ten minutes. A computer system eliminates all the paperwork and duplicated effort of traditional loan processing.

When a "telephone banker" types the first few identifying details of a loan application into a computer, the machine automatically finds the records of the customer's previous activity with the bank. Simultaneously, it orders an electronic version of the applicant's credit-bureau file. The Personal Banker then contacts by pager one of two loan officers, who searches for records of the customer's banking and credit history. A loan officer can then make a decision in less than a minute. In 1993, after its first year in operation with the new computer-telephone loan system, Huntington Bancshares received 1.1 million phone calls and opened 75,000 new accounts, nearly triple the rate under traditional face-to-face contact between customer and loan officer.

"... if you plan to expand into the full range of traditional and nontraditional financial services, they [automated banking services] will be the key to our customer relationships."

"We see our automated banking systems as both a link and an extension of our ongoing personal-banker activities," says Richard L. Stage, executive vice president of consumer services for Huntington Bancshares.

"Customers increasingly want to do banking whenever and wherever they are," says W. Lee Hoskins, president and chief executive officer of The Huntington National Bank. Telecommunications and computers help to provide these services.

Computer-telephone automated banking appears to be the way of the future. "If you are just going to do traditional banking in branches, then perhaps they will be dinosaurs," says John Russell, chief communications officer of the Banc One Corporation, Huntington's main competitor in Columbus. "But if you plan to expand into the full range of traditional and nontraditional financial services, they [automated banking services] will be the key to our customer relationships."

# 11

# Law Enforcement

T he applications of computers and other information technology in law and law enforcement are varied and often
very exciting. For instance, during the 1994 Winter Olympic Games, some 2,000 IBM PS/2 personal computers
were installed in Lillehammer, Norway. They not only kept
the scores, provided instant sports results to media all over the world,
and tracked weather and air-pollution counts but they substantially
reduced the number of police needed to patrol the vast Olympic
sites. The desktop computers replaced banks of bulkier and much
more expensive mainframe computers that have been used for more
than two decades at Olympic games.

International Business Machines Corporation provided the
hardware, while consultants from Chicago-based Arthur Andersen
Consulting provided the software and assembled the computer
network at the Norwegian games. They developed a system called
Info 92 that linked remote terminals to a central database.

Using computer-network techniques, more police coverage was
provided with fewer police. Dispatchers in each of 13 sporting-event
locations were linked by desktop computers. They, in turn, kept in
contact with all foot and squad patrols through the U.S. Pentagon's
Global Positioning Satellite System. The system was designed to

Police are using computers and telecommunications in many aspects of their work.
(Photo courtesy IBM)

allow military units and others, such as airplane pilots, to bounce signals off a satellite and obtain their location anywhere on earth within only a few feet.

The satellites tracked the movements of every police officer assigned to the Olympics. That information was constantly updated on the dispatchers' computer screens across the entire Olympics playing area. Whenever an incident occurred that required police attention, a dispatcher could identify the nearest patrol at a glance, then make contact with officers by simply clicking a mouse pointer on an icon on their computer screen. Computers could also recognize whether the closest officer or squad had the proper equipment, or even enough experience, to respond to a given call.

In past Olympics, policing was done through telephone and radio equipment rather than computers. There was really no way to use mainframes in hands-on police operations. A big advantage of

> Whenever an incident occurred that required police attention, a dispatcher could identify the nearest patrol at a glance, then make contact with officers by simply clicking a mouse pointer on an icon on their computer screen.

knowing each officer's location by computer at any given moment is that dispatchers can guarantee a timely response with a much smaller pool of police and squad cars. Policing by computer reduced police patrols by 500 people, from the 3,500 officers who would have been needed to cover the 40,000 square miles of games without client/server computing to just 3,000.

The success of the computerized policing at the Norway Olympics suggests that budget-strapped cities around the nation and the world may apply the technology to their police departments. It could reduce staffs and at the same time increase efficiency.

Some uses of computers in police work are even more dramatic than the Olympics example. Each year, 4,500 children are kidnapped or otherwise disappear in the United States. In the past, a photo of the missing child might appear on telephone poles or in post offices or mailings in a community. Today, the photo can be sent along the rapidly growing information superhighway onto home-computer screens across the nation. By generating an electronic poster bearing a photo of the child and an FBI sketch of the possible kidnapper, police can send their images to computer screens and over fax machines to many more thousands of people who might be of help in finding the missing child.

The first application of this type of computer-aided police work was the brainchild of three California residents. They used the system in 1993 to help police find a missing 12-year-old girl who was kidnapped from her home in Petaluma, north of San Francisco. She had apparently been taken off by a bearded knife-wielding stranger who had invaded her slumber party.

When he learned of the kidnapping, Gary French, an unemployed computer-systems salesman, offered police his help. As he watched a fax machine slowly turn out poor reproductions of a suspect's sketch, he thought, "We can do this all electronically." With the help of Bill Rhodes, owner of a local print shop, and Larry Magid, a syndicated computer columnist, they scanned a photo of the girl and a police artist's sketch of the suspected kidnapper. The images were sent out over computer networks, including the Internet, which, in turn, transmitted them to 250 computer bulletin boards across the nation. Several computer companies then donated eight computers that were put to use faxing 1,000 posters a minute to grocery chains and other locations. Two nationwide instant-print shops, PIP and Kinko's, pitched in to convert the electronic images into high-quality hard copies at all their outlets. Local volunteers distributed the posters. Unfortunately, the story does not have a happy ending, since the girl was later found dead. Her abductor and killer was, however, later arrested.

On the positive side, these efforts laid the groundwork for lightning-fast electronic searches for other missing children. To help accomplish this, a national directory of fax numbers was fed into a permanent database for the National Center for Missing and Exploited Children in Arlington, Virginia. Magid, meanwhile, hopes that computer networks can be the equivalent of a 911 phone number for missing-persons emergencies. With these systems in place, missing children could have millions of searchers looking for them.

# 12

# Marketing

M arketing means finding out what potential customers for your product or service want, and then selling it to them. The process of marketing can involve researching, advertising, shipping, storing, and selling. Computers and video recorders are proving to be very helpful tools in learning more about potential customers.

In one example of marketing, Chilton Research Services, a market-research company in Radnor, Pennsylvania, is offering an innovative survey method called Right There Research. The program puts handheld 8-millimeter video cameras into the hands of consumers, who tape themselves in such everyday situations as shopping, eating, driving, and working.

On the surface, it would appear that the idea is to let people test-use the video cameras so they will buy them. In fact, selling the camera is not the intended end result of the program. Learning about the person is. The videotapes people make of themselves reveal more accurate personal information about their behavior as consumers than traditional research methods do.

"Companies struggling to define their markets can have an 'Aha!' experience about who their customers are," says Richard Luker, a research account executive at Chilton.

Computerized market-research systems help locate and identify potential customers.
(Photo courtesy IBM)

For instance, footage from the video experiment revealed one woman's preference for dessert toppings. She videotaped an expedition into her refrigerator in which she held up a can of Reddi Whip and declared to the camera, "This is whipped cream. I only like the real stuff. I don't like the Cool Whips."

The videotaping helped marketing researchers at DDB Needham in Los Angeles learn a lot. They gave video cameras to young men ages 16 to 19 to track their reactions as blue jeans consumers for their client, Bugle Boy Industries.

"It gave us real insight by allowing us to look at them functioning in their everyday, natural lives," says Candy Deemer, a Needham vice president. "While the tapes confirmed what we already knew, about things like comfort, it was surprising to hear the young men say, 'I got these at 50 percent off.' So price was important to them."

The favorite line from the blue-jeans videos was from one teenage boy who doesn't believe in hanging up any of his clothes. He said, "Your closet is where old clothes go to die."

The videotapes helped Needham develop a Bugle Boy television commercial and spawned another marketing test: videotaping the life of a cold.

Meanwhile, the use of multimedia in marketing research is helping Visual Research Communications (VRC) of Metuchen, New Jersey, gather consumer opinion to guide the development of clients' products and services. The company produces "Video Reports" of research findings using desktop video equipment and computers.

"Our video reports are important to clients because they think of video as a true communications tool," says Kevin Lonnie, cofounder of VRC. "It validates the quality of their research throughout the organization and more people can be influenced by it."

The Super-VHS video format was used because it produces industrial-quality video for a reasonable price. The Amiga computer was selected because it runs the Video Toaster software that creates video productions for far less than the cost of video-production studio equipment.

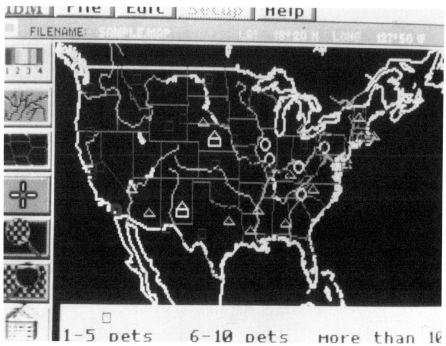

Computer software identifies pet owners for market-research study by pet-food company.

"The Toaster gave us the look of television, the pizzazz, the special effects," says Riccardo Lopez, Lonnie's partner. "People get used to special effects on TV and expect to see them in a quality production. With the Toaster, we give them the perception that we spent a lot of money producing the video."

The company also uses desktop video to market itself, taking a videotape of its services to potential clients.

"Video was our passion," says Lonnie, "until we recently began switching to CD-ROM production and multimedia presentations. Our first venture into CD-ROM was to design a marketing strategy using the technology for one of the leading communications corporations. They wanted random access to information segments so their employees could pick through the information packed onto the CD."

Now the marketing company is designing interactive CDs. Users can be presented with statistical information and can input their own numbers to witness what effect it has on tracking research by graphs.

Changes in the field of communications technology for marketing research are rapid, as Lonnie explains: "As CD-ROMs work their way into the workplace, and more powerful desktop personal computers are on more people's desks, marketing people can take advantage of the digital revolution. Reports that had been prepared on videotape will be prepared on CD-ROM. Videotape, as a marketing tool, will start to fade out, the way eight-tracks lost out to audiocassettes."

> "Our video reports are important to clients because they think of video as a true communications tool."

> "People get used to special effects on TV and expect to see them in a quality production. With the Toaster, we give them the perception that we spent a lot of money producing the video."

Meanwhile, since information is one of the keys to marketing, gathering data on prospective customers has been speeded up and made more accurate by the use of computer and telecommunications networking. Marketing researchers gain access to vast databases of consumer information by using World-Wide Web, a system for linking information through the Internet's international network of computers. Together with systems such as Netscape and Homepages, market researchers have access to sound, graphics, and text not available through traditional Internet connections.

# Publishing

S ome of the most fastest-moving effects of computeriza-
tion and other technology on the new information superhighway are being felt in the newspaper, magazine,
and book-publishing industries. Is the new publishing
destination for readers to be electronic newspapers,
magazines, and books?

Rapid development of electronic information technologies such
as on-line, fax, and modem data-retrieval
services are having a significant impact on
the $45 billion newspaper industry.
Newspaper companies are racing toward
electronic media of all kinds in an attempt
to counter competition.

Reporters at many newspapers across
the nation switched from using typewriters
to computers more than a decade ago, and
newspaper morgues (libraries containing
articles from back issues) were converted
into computer files. Linotype machines
were put out to pasture, replaced by new
computer-operated printing presses.

> In some cases, entire electronic editions of papers have supplemented, though not replaced, traditional "paper" newspapers.

Production supervisors use power computers to keep track of various stages of book publication.
(Photo courtesy IBM)

The next step has been for newspapers to go on-line, offering computer-fax-modem services to readers. In some cases, entire electronic editions of papers have supplemented, though not re-placed, traditional "paper" newspapers.

Increasingly, newspaper executives and industry analysts recognize that computer, telephone, and cable hookups can enable them to compete successfully and inexpensively in the sale of electronic news and other information.

"With the digital age fast approaching, the newspaper industry has been racking its communal brains figuring out how not to be left behind," says Tod A. Jacobs, a newspaper securities analyst at Sanford C. Bernstein & Company.

The *Chicago Tribune* began Chicago Online in 1992 to become the first electronic newspaper on a national on-line service, America Online. Since then about 60 daily papers, including most of the

nation's largest, have begun offering electronic services of some sort, from headline news to financial and sports news. At least 28 daily papers are working in partnership with one or another of the five major on-line services: America Online, Prodigy, Compuserve, Delphi Internet Services, and the Interchange Online Network. The papers include the *New York Times*, the *Washington Post*, the *Los Angeles Times*, the *Philadelphia Inquirer*, and the *St. Louis Post-Dispatch*.

> Newspapers face an uncertain future because of fierce competition from television news and on-line news services.

Newspapers face an uncertain future because of fierce competition from television news and on-line news services. Many loyal readers who for years bought the daily paper as a matter of habit are reading less and tuning in to electronic sources for the news they want.

How newspapers react to and face electronic competition is still an open question, but one response is to print international editions. The *Miami Herald*, for instance, publishes both Latin American and South American editions, transmitting pages via satellite to printing plants in Peru and other countries.

Magazines, similarly searching for ways to stay alive in the electronic information age, are joining on-line services and producing CD-ROM editions.

The approach some magazine publishers are taking to solving the electronic dilemma is to offer their readers interactive services. *Time* magazine became the first newsmagazine to enter the interactive network age when it started Time Online in 1993. For the price of an America Online subscription ($9.95 a month plus $3.50 an hour after the first five hours each month), computer users receive the text of each new issue of *Time* magazine on their monitors by 4 p.m. each Sunday. Readers can browse through the electronic magazine or scan back issues.

Time Online is a two-way street. Readers can send messages to *Time* editors with the click of a computer mouse. Communications

> Users can browse through text, graphics, and animated images, and can even receive voice recordings from radio interviews gathered from the magazine's weekly program, "Newsweek on Air."

appear on an electronic bulletin board that staff members and other subscribers can read and respond to. On-line forums bring subscribers and newsmakers together. "This brings all of us into the large and rapidly expanding interactive computer culture," says Richard Duncan, supervisor of Time Online.

An example of a magazine available on CD-ROM is *Newsweek*, which offers a quarterly version of the magazine for computers equipped with CD-ROM drives. Users can browse through text, graphics, and animated images, and can even receive voice recordings from radio interviews gathered from the magazine's weekly program, "Newsweek on Air." Each CD-ROM issue also includes a text archive of three months of the magazine's articles, searchable by keyword.

Johann Gutenberg, the German printer who invented the movable-type printing press in about 1436, would not recognize book-publishing methods today, as books, too, are actively engaged in the new information age. A new generation of digital printing presses is emerging that eliminates the need for metal plates, creating flexibility that allows shorter press runs and almost instant changes.

Many book publishers are also putting out CD-ROM editions with multimedia and interactive capabilities. The entire 24-volume Grolier encyclopedia is available on a single disc—a disc that includes graphics and dozens of color animations and sound movies that are not available in the printed books.

Book publishers also are taking advantage of the high interest many computer users have in getting their information from on-line services. Some are starting to work with on-line companies to promote their books and allow readers to interact with their authors in literary discussions. In some cases, publishers are selling electronic editions of their books whose words pop up on users' computer screens. One book publisher recently sold the first serial rights to Stephen King's new book, *Nightmares and Dreamscapes*, not to a magazine but to the On-Line Book Store, a service that makes books available to on-line customers.

Some book publishers are setting up electronic author tours whereby on-line users can take part in readers' forums about and with their favorite writers. It is as if writers and readers were having a literary discussion over dinner.

No one is predicting that CD-ROM discs or on-line systems will replace books in paper form. But publishers are finding that these services can be effective in drawing attention to literature. The development comes at a time when reading is increasingly competing with cable and satellite television and video-game technologies for the public's attention.

Are newspapers, magazines, and books endangered species, fated to become extinct like the dodo bird? Don't bet on it, say publishers.

In its 1993 debut edition, *Wired*, a magazine dedicated to the "digital generation," the editor predicted that the communications revolution would "whip through our lives like a typhoon." It could create "social changes so profound that their only parallel is probably the discovery of fire."

In its second edition, however, *Wired* published an article by Paul Saffo, a fellow at the Institute for the Future in Menlo Park, California. "*Litera scripta manet*," wrote the futurist, quoting the Roman poet Horace. "The written word remains. We talk endlessly about new tech-arcana like video and virtual reality. But the conversation orbits around the stuff of this page—text. In fact, the written word doesn't just remain; it is flourishing like kudzu vines at the boundaries of the digital revolution."

David Bunnell, the founder of NewMedia, another new magazine covering digital technologies, agrees: "Computer screens are good for some things, like electronic mail and data bases. But for now, it's just not clear that you can make text on a screen be as beautiful and accessible as it is on paper."

"When you use multimedia—audio and video—too much, you're just reinventing television," says Michael Rogers, managing editor of *Newsweek Interactive*, one of the first magazines to appear on CD-ROM. "Now people are starting to appreciate text again. For the pure power of ideas, there's nothing like text, and ideas are one of those things that move us as humans. I tell my programmers 'text is intellectual data compression, and it's a real cool thing.'"

Then, too, a CD-ROM disc of a book, lying on a coffee table, is a dead thing without a computer. It can't hold a candle to its book edition, sitting there waiting to be read. An avid book reader friend says, "I can't see anyone ever saying, 'You can't tell a CD-ROM by its cover!'"

# 14

# Retailing

E lectronic technology has had a major impact on retailing—selling of goods directly to customers. You can still buy goods at a store where a salesperson waits on you. You can still buy from direct-mail flyers and catalogs, placing your order by mail or telephone. But these are old-fashioned ways of buying.

Today you can do your grocery shopping from home by accessing Peapod, an interactive home-shopping service that allows you to shop from your personal computer and modem. For a small service charge, you can learn about sale items and place your complete order by computer, then have it delivered to your home. Ameritech recently bought an interest in Peapod, an Evanston, Illinois–based company, to expand on-line grocery shopping nationally.

More exciting, you can shop and buy through one of several interactive home-shopping channels over cable television. A saleswoman will model a dress or a diamond necklace, or a salesman will demonstrate riding an exercise bike. By modem, fax, or telephone, you can order whatever the teleshopping channels show you.

Old-fashioned paper catalogs are being replaced by CD-ROM discs that demonstrate products in color and sound movies. There are even CD-ROM collections of catalogs.

These are just a few of the ways retailers now reach potential customers. They've come a long way from the traveling salesman who came to your door with a suitcase display of new watches. The stakes are very high, as teleretailing grows into a multibillion-dollar business.

Late in 1994, Montgomery Ward, one of the nation's largest retail store chains, formerly known for its huge seasonal catalogs, entered the television-shopping race. It invested a relatively small

Department stores use video programs to inform customers about products and sales.
(Photo courtesy IBM)

$8 million to buy a small share in Value Vision International, the nation's third-largest home-shopping network. This network reaches about 24 million homes through Time Warner, one of the largest cable television operators. Montgomery Ward started by selling its big-ticket items like home appliances, electronics, furniture, and home-office equipment over the home-shopping network. The investment seems likely to pay off—since in the first test, of only 12 minutes' duration on a Saturday morning, 32 Apple computers were sold at $2,000 per unit.

In another move, MCI Communications, one of the nation's leading long-distance telephone companies, has begun operating an "electronic shopping mall" for consumers over the Internet. MCI plans to sell personal-computer software that will let people shop at electronic storefronts and order goods through the computer by credit card.

Studies reveal, however, that at least so far, most people have not taken to electronic shopping. A 1994 Times Mirror study reported that although 29 percent of people surveyed said they had seen a home-shopping channel, only 10 percent of those said they bought merchandise that way.

Similarly, a Louis Harris poll revealed that while most Americans show a high interest in the educational and communications aspects of the emerging national information system, they are not as interested in the interactive entertainment or home-shopping features. Out of 1,000 adults sampled, 68 percent said they were not interested in shopping for and buying goods and services through home-shopping channels that combine cable television, telephone, and computer networks. Many consumers said they are concerned about the potential abuse of personal information gleaned from households by advertisers and other interactive service providers.

> Many consumers said they are concerned about the potential abuse of personal information gleaned from households by advertisers and other interactive service providers.

The prospects for on-line shopping will probably brighten as more customers become convinced that their privacy will be assured. Retail analysts are working on this and other problems to make teleshopping more attractive to consumers.

# 15

# Television

M any "techies"—people who keep up with the latest in electronic technology and buy the newest audio-video products as soon as they are available—say they have seen the future of television and it is satellite. Having seen satellite television myself, I agree. It is the most exciting thing in television since color came along in the 1960s.

Nothing so far, not even laser discs, which until now put out the sharpest picture and the best sound, compares with the clarity of satellite television broadcasts, even on projection TV sets as large as 45 inches diagonally. Televised professional football games look as though they are being played in your living room. Movies show so sharp and with such depth they appear to be three-dimensional.

Receiving television signals from satellites used to require a huge dish that cost at least $2,500. But in the spring of 1994, Thomson Consumer Electronics, the French owner of the RCA television business, introduced its Digital Satellite System (DSS) with a smaller receiving dish, only 18 inches in diameter, for about $700. DSS was initially intended to be bought by those in rural areas—about 12 million people who are not served by cable television. As sales took off much faster than expected, though, it soon became apparent that even many people living in cities and suburbs were eager to switch

"Small dish" TV antennas receive sharp pictures and clear sound from space-based satellites.
(Photo courtesy RCA)

from cable to satellite, for the laser-quality picture and compact-disc–like sound.

While we wait for high-definition television (HDTV) to get here, five to ten years or more into the future, DSS provides the sharpest television reception yet possible. Like cable TV, the satellite system also gives strong competition to video rental stores, because viewers can order movies, concerts, or sporting events of their choice to be telecast onto their home TV screens without going to the store. Satellite home-viewing offers many more choices than are offered by cable. Also, while cable offers viewers over 30 channels, DSS provides 150 and can expand to 500.

■ ■ ■

As for the long-promised arrival of HDTV, to provide a super-sharp picture, the television industry and consumers are still waiting for the Federal Communications Commission to agree on a high-definition television standard for the United States.

"The new digital standard will open a door to profound changes in the way we interact with the rest of the world through our televisions," predicts James M. Barry, editor of *Video* magazine. Some HDTV is expected to be broadcast at the 1996 Summer Olympics Games in Atlanta, Georgia, but the first HDTV sets may cost from $7,000 to $10,000.

"The new digital standard will open a door to profound changes in the way we interact with the rest of the world through our television."

"Digital television is essentially a computer that can be equipped with the electronic memory and processing power to send, store, and manipulate images at high speed," says Edmund L. Andrews, technology writer for the *New York Times*. "If, in the future, homes are linked by high-speed optical fibers, digital television sets will be able to evolve smoothly from passive viewing boxes to tools."

HDTV might be used to roam through remote libraries, retrieving movies or electronic books that combine written text, databases, and video. Or it could be used as a tool in telecommuting, enabling employees to work at home and use their television sets to send data and hold video conferences. HDTV also has applications in factory automation, medical imaging, even defense, with satellite and radar telecommunications.

"Digital is going to change the world of home electronics. The possibilities are limited only by the bounds of your imagination."

"High-definition is the least interesting thing about the next generation of TV," says Michael Bove, associate professor at Massachusetts Institute of Technology's Media Lab. "The interesting part is that it will put a computer into your TV."

"Digital is going to change the world of home electronics," agrees James McKinney, chairman of the Advanced Television Systems Committee, an industry group that is working out production standards for the new television. "The possibilities are limited only by the bounds of your imagination."

Many of us—not just techies—can hardly wait.

# 16

# But What About Privacy?

hile everyone from aerospace engineers to zipper makers uses computer networking and telecommunications to roll merrily up and down the new information superhighway, at least one major concern has arisen: the question of privacy. With the creation of thousands of data banks (computerized lists of names, addresses, and phone numbers) including virtually everyone in the United States, and electronic bulletin boards that dispense and share names and information, businesspeople and private citizens are beginning to wonder how they can be assured that they will not be exploited, or that what they know will not be misused, perhaps against them.

Early in 1993, the Clinton administration encouraged the development of an information superhighway to electronically connect all aspects of American business and leisure life via computers, telephones, and other technology. The following spring, however, it took another step when it pressed Congress for legislation that would amount to government and/or police being able to eavesdrop on those using the technology. Some called it a form of wiretapping (electronic monitoring of telephone calls). Legislation would be enacted to force telephone and cable television companies to install computer software on their

Government and industry efforts are ongoing to assure privacy in networking.
(Photo courtesy IBM))

networks that would enable law-enforcement agencies to eavesdrop on phone calls and computer transmissions. The proposed legislation came at the same time the administration was promoting the use of an eavesdropping computer chip, known as the "Clipper chip." Designed by National Security Agency scientists, it would help police and other law-enforcement agencies intercept coded computer communications.

The proposed legislation was a revised version of a similar measure proposed earlier by the Bush administration. While it would not change any of the legal standards set for law-enforcement agencies' wiretaps, it would require companies to install technology that makes it possible to continue traditional wiretapping.

Telecommunications companies and civil-rights groups protested the proposed new legislation and the eavesdropping chip. Telephone companies said it would cost their industry millions of dollars to make and install eavesdropping devices, and civil-rights groups argued that the efforts posed potential threats to privacy.

"We're not objecting to wiretaps," said Marc Rotenberg, director of Computer Professionals for Social Responsibility, a nonprofit group in Washington. "We're saying they don't have the right to pass a law that requires people to make it easier to wiretap."

Further fears were voiced by other nonprofit organizations, such as the Electronic Frontier Foundation in Washington. "We're not only talking about voice communications," said Jerry Berman, executive director of the group. "Wiretapping technology would access information on what kind of movies we watch, what kind of commerce we engage in, what kind of political parties we want to communicate with. All of these things are going to be on the information highway."

> Legislation would be enacted to force telephone and cable television companies to install computer software on their networks that would enable law-enforcement agencies to eavesdrop on phone calls and computer transmissions.

After several months of opposition, the administration began considering alternatives to both the proposed legislation and the wiretapping chip. No further developments had been reported when this book went into production late in 1995.

However, another privacy concern surfaced along the information superhighway at about the same time as the wiretap controversy—this one about a federal proposal to establish a computerized registry. It would be a data bank of all U.S. citizens, linked to their Social Security numbers, and would include as well all immigrants authorized to work in this country, so that employers would be able to determine every job applicant's identity. "This could bring us perilously close to having an internal passport system," cautioned Ira Glasser, executive director of the American Civil Liberties Union.

While many benefits are to be seen in the wider gathering and dissemination of information through computers and tele-communications, a major fear persists among many that the technology makes it too easy to invade people's privacy and to acquire information on how business and industry conduct their work. Civil-rights groups argue that it is too easy to use the power of the computer and other technology to find personal and possibly damaging information about people. An example is an insurance company's data bank of information on policyholders. Who knows if data on a particular person, regarding his or her driving record, medical or financial history, or other personal information, is accurate? Also, professionals using on-line networks for obtaining and sharing information related to their work are concerned that knowledge they might wish to be kept private could be illegally or unfairly used by others using the same technology.

As the information superhighway expands and more people use the technology available, concerns regarding the accuracy and confidentiality of information, and about an individual's personal and professional privacy, are likely to remain significant.

A related concern is copyright protection in the information age, as computer and computer-network users can easily copy and disseminate text, pictures, sound, and video images that exist in digital form. The Commerce Department is studying the possibility of rewriting the copyright laws to protect the creators of books, recordings, movies, and other forms of information in the digital age.

> "Wiretapping technology would access information on what kind of movies we watch, what kind of commerce we engage in, what kind of political parties we want to communicate with. All of these things are going to be on the information highway."

Meanwhile, the Folio Corporation of Provo, Utah, has devised a new system for electronic publishing that could allow information providers to sell copyrighted articles and graphics over the Internet and other wide-area networks.

# 17

# The Future of Technology in Business and Industry

M any on the leading edge of technology in the workplace predict that the company of the future will be plugged in to new technologies undreamed of even today. One of these forecasters, John A. Byrne of New York City, writing in *Business Week* magazine, has described the ultimate in adaptability—"the virtual corporation."

"The virtual corporation is a temporary network of independent companies—suppliers, customers, even erstwhile rivals—linked by information technology to share skills, costs, and access to one another's markets," says Byrne. "It will have neither central office nor organization chart. It will have no hierarchy, no vertical integration."

Instead, Byrne predicts, the new, evolving corporate model will be fluid and flexible, a group of collaborators that quickly unites to exploit a specific business opportunity. Once the specific goal has been met, the venture will, more often than not, disband. "It's not just a good idea,

The future for technology in business looks bright since, historically, technology creates more jobs than it causes to be lost. (Photo courtesy IBM)

it's inevitable," agrees Gerald Ross, co-founder of Change Lab International, a consulting firm in Greenwich, Connecticut.

Not only technology but partnerships will make virtual corporations possible. "Partnering—the key attribute of the virtual corporation—will assume even greater importance," says James R. Houghton, chairman of Corning, Inc., one of the nation's leading examples of corporate alliances. Its 19 partnerships have enabled the company to develop and sell new products faster. "More companies are waking up to the fact that alliances are critical to the future. Technologies are changing so fast that nobody can do it all alone anymore."

Byrne says today's joint ventures are little more than early glimpses of the highly adaptable, opportunistic structures of the future.

"When we talk about virtual corporations today, we're mainly talking about alliances and outsourcing agreements," says John Sculley, chairman of Apple Computer, Inc. Many businesses today,

> "More companies are waking up to the fact that alliances are critical to the future. Technologies are changing so fast that nobody can do it all alone anymore."

and even more in the future, will sign contracts with various other companies to provide specific services. Together, they make a whole product, in much the same way that home-building contractors sign subcontracting agreements with manufacturers of windows, heating and cooling systems, or kitchen and bath supplies. Together, they build a house.

"Ten or twenty years from now, you'll see an explosion of entrepreneurial industries and companies that will essentially form the real virtual corporations," says Sculley. "Tens of thousands of virtual organizations may come out of this."

Roger N. Nagel, operations director for Lehigh University's Iacocca Institute in Bethlehem, Pennsylvania, envisions a business world of the future in which information technology could make the creation of virtual enterprises "as straightforward as connecting components for a home audio and video system by different manufacturers." He foresees a national information infrastructure linking computers and machine tools across the United States. This communications superhighway would permit the far-flung units of different companies to quickly locate suppliers, designers, and manufacturers through an information clearinghouse.

Teams of people in different companies would routinely work together, via computer networks, in real time. Artificial intelligence systems and sensing devices would connect engineers directly to the production line.

Some industry leaders are skeptical of the concept of the virtual corporation, fearing that companies that join a network of companies could lose control over their product or their management. Others, such as labor leaders, fear that the virtual corporation could mean the loss of more lower- or middle-management jobs, and the farming out of jobs to low-wage countries.

Advances in information technology will play a central role in the development of the virtual corporation. New generations of digital office equipment are already being manufactured by Xerox and other companies that will transform the way work is done in offices. New digital products will scan paper documents, store their contents, print them on demand, and send them via modem or fax almost instantly anywhere in the world.

Scientists at the NEC Corporation in Japan have already made the world's thinnest wires, with a diameter the width of several atoms. They could pave the way for ultrafine electronic circuitry in computers and telecommunications.

> "People in business would like to buy a very fat pipe through which they can pump everything—voice, data, video, E-Mail, and faxes—rather than using separate connections."

Vinton Cerf, "the father of the Internet," is working on new technology to further revolutionize information gathering and dissemination. "People in business would like to buy a very fat pipe through which they can pump everything—voice, data, video, E-Mail, and faxes—rather than using separate connections," says Cerf. He is working to create just such an electronic "pipe."

Many diverse voices are describing what the future of information technology will be in business and industry, science and medicine, education, entertainment, and other fields. One common vision emerges. The merging of computer, telephone, television, and other technologies on the information superhighway, and their multimedia and interactive capabilities, together with advances in wireless and digital transmission, will change the way people around the world live, work, and play. Most believe the change will be for the better.

# GLOSSARY

| | |
|---|---|
| **analog information transmission** | A method of storing information, typically sound or motion video, as continuously varying wave forms. |
| **bulletin boards (computer)** | Telecommunications services that allow computer users to send or receive messages. |
| **circuit** | A circular stream of electricity. |
| **CD** | Compact disc. An information-recording medium for digital sound. |
| **CD-I** | Compact disc with interactive capabilities. |
| **CD-ROM** | Compact disc read-only memory. A 4.75-inch laser-encoded optical disc that stores but cannot record data. |
| **chip (computer)** | A computer circuit built on a small piece, or chip, of semiconductor material. |
| **data** | Information that can be processed by a computer. |
| **database** | A collection of data, sometimes called a database management system, that stores, retrieves, organizes, and reports on data stored on a computer. |
| **digital information transmission** | A method of recording information electronically in numeric units. |
| **disk drive** | The part of a computer that "reads" the information stored on a disc or "floppy disk." |

| | |
|---|---|
| **distance learning** | Information that is obtained via telephone, television, computer, or an other electronic source that comes from a distant location. |
| **electronic mail ("E-Mail")** | Messages sent electronically to and from different computers via the computer network. |
| **fax (facsimile transmission)** | An electronic method of sending and receiving printed information. A document is converted into a series of lines of electrical information that is transmitted by telephone. |
| **fiber-optic cable** | A cable made from a bundle of fine glass strands over which information is transmitted in the form of an intense beam of light. |
| **graphics** | Computer-generated art and illustrations. |
| **hard drive** | An internal drive in a computer system unit that houses a permanently installed hard or fixed drive that stores the information put into the computer. |
| **high-definition television (HDTV)** | A digital television broadcasting system that can create sharper, clearer pictures than regular television produces. |
| **hologram** | A three-dimensional photograph taken by laser. |
| **icon** | A small on-screen picture or graphic that symbolizes a specific computer activity or program. |
| **information superhighway** | Term used to describe a vast network of shared information via computer, television, satellite, and other forms of communication. |
| **interactive** | The ability to offer many choices that result in succeeding scenarios that vary according to the choices made by the operator. |
| **interactive multimedia** | Various types of information devices presented interactively by a computer in response to user input. |

| | |
|---|---|
| Internet | An international information network accessible by use of a computer, modem, and telephone. |
| ISDN (Integrated Systems Digital Network) | An international standard for transmission of digital data over telephone lines. |
| laser | A device that produces a very pure and intense light, used in various ways for information storage and optics. |
| laser disc | An optical storage disc, typically 12 inches in diameter, that carries video, audio, and text to be played back on a TV set or video monitor. Also known as a videodisc. |
| laser disc player | Like a video recorder (VCR) except that instead of tapes, it plays laser discs that produce sharper images and CD-quality sound, provide swift random playback to any location on the disc, and store vast amounts of images. |
| letterbox | (See WIDESCREEN). |
| LAN (Local Area Network) | A linked group of computers, typically connected by cables, that supports the sharing of files and applications among users. A school's LAN includes all the computers in the school that are hooked together to share software and administrative tools. |
| megabytes | A numerical measure of the number of characters the computer can handle at once. "Mega" means million, and one megabyte equals about 500 pages of text. |
| modem (modulator-demodulator) | A computer accessory that translates computer data into a series of tones transmitted over telephone lines for sending and receiving text and graphics. |
| monitor | A computer screen. |

| | |
|---|---|
| **multimedia** | The combination of sound, still and moving visuals, and text in one on-screen computer application. |
| **network** | A system of interconnected pieces of equipment such as radios, telephones, television transmitters, or computers that can communicate with one another and share the same software, information, and related equipment such as printers. |
| **on-line** | To be available on a computer network. |
| **optical fibers** | Fine strands of glass used to carry light from lasers. |
| **RAM (random access memory)** | A way to measure how much information the computer's memory can hold and work with. |
| **scanner** | A computer accessory that captures images so they can be used in a computer application. |
| **simulation** | A multimedia application that is designed to simulate a real-world environment. |
| **software** | Computer programs that can perform various tasks. |
| **spreadsheet** | A software program that enables computer users to conduct mathematical calculations such as budgeting, keeping track of investments, or tracking grades. |
| **telecommunications** | A means of communicating with people in other locations through the use of a combination of computer software, modems, and telephone lines. |
| **teleconference** | A method by which people in different places are able to communicate via shared television channels. |
| **3DO** | A machine similar in appearance to a CD or laser-disc player that plays interactive multimedia discs |

| | |
|---|---|
| | with expanded capabilities of image sharpness and greater animation speed. |
| **virtual reality** | Computer or other electronic software that allows users to experience a simulated environment that they seem to physically enter. |
| **WAN (wide-area network)** | A network spanning a large geographic area, such as a multischool district or an entire state. Local networks can connect or dial in. |
| **widescreen** | Television sets that show movies not in the square format of standard TV screens but in the wider ratio seen on movie-theater screens. (Also called "letterbox.") |
| **word processing** | Typing and editing manuscripts with a computer, using special software. |

# SOURCES

## STUDIES/REPORTS

*The Role of Technology in American Life.* Times Mirror Center for the People & the Press, Washington, D.C., 1994.
*Across the Atlantic.* Robert Half International, Menlo Park, California, 1993.
Louis Harris & Associates, 1994.
Link Resources, New York City, 1994.

## PERIODICALS

Barry, James M. "Why Not the Best?" *Video*, July 1993.
Droegemueller, Lee. "Connecting with the Future Today." *T.H.E. Journal*, April 1994, p. 10.
Hines, Andy. "Jobs and Infotech." *The Futurist*, January–February 1994, pp. 9–13.
Lehtinen, Rick. "Desktop Video." *Video Pro*, April 1994, pp. 36–49.
Levy, Steven. "TechnoMania." *Newsweek*, February 27, 1995, pp. 13, 26.
Richman, Louis S. "The New Worker Elite." *Fortune*, August 22, 1994, pp. 56–66.

## NEWSPAPERS

Bane, Michael. "Hidden Costs Rise as PCs Spread." *Chicago Tribune*, March 14, 1993, p. B1.
Calem, Robert E. "Desktop Computers Reshaping the Way Ads Are Made." *New York Times*, June 19, 1994, p. F9.
Coates, James. "Computerized Policing an Olympic Winner." *Chicago Tribune*, February 27, 1994, Sec. 7, p. 3.

Cotter, Holland. "The Gentle Art of Those Who Preserve Art." *New York Times*, October 17, 1994, p. B1.

Elliott, Stuart. "Advertising." *New York Times*, December 2, 1994, p. C16, and August 23, 1993, p. C15.

Fiorini, Phillip. "AT&T Telecommuting a Hit." *USA Today*, September 21, 1994, p. B1.

Glaberson, William. "Press Notes." *New York Times*, October 10, 1994, p. C5.

Holusha, John. "Steel Rivals Join to Study New Method." *New York Times*, October 11, 1994, p. C1.

Johnson, Kirk. "At I.B.M., Desk Sharing and No Frills." *New York Times*, March 14, 1994, p. A9.

Kleiman, Carol. "Brain Power Will Propel Future." *Chicago Tribune*, July 17, 1994, p. B1.

Kruger, Pamela. "The Multimedia Job Miracle." *New York Times*, January 9, 1994, p. F9.

Malone, Michael S. "The Conference Rooms at the Cyberspace Inn." *New York Times*, May 29, 1994, p. F21.

O'Brien, Timothy L. "A PC Revolution." *Wall Street Journal*, October 8, 1993, p. 1.

Race, Tim. "Testing the Telecommute." *Chicago Tribune*, August 8, 1993.

Wald, Matthew L. "Aided by Computers, Repairs Are Charted." *New York Times*, March 8, 1993, p. A12.

Weber, Thomas E. "Wanted: Genius." *Wall Street Journal*, May 24, 1993, p. R9.

Young, Lucie. "For More People, Home Is Where the Work Is." *New York Times*, September 29, 1994, p. B1.

## INTERVIEWS

Bower, Art. Telephone conversation, October 1, 1994.
Baurac, David. Telephone conversation, November 7, 1994.
Campbell, Jean. Telephone conversation, May 25, 1994.
DiCiara, Robert. Telephone conversation, December 5, 1994.
Drombrowski, Todd. Telephone conversation, August 10, 1994.
Eichenberger, Jean. Telephone conversation, August 1, 1994.
Face, Sally. Telephone conversation, November 20, 1994.
French, Gary. Telephone conversation, December 8, 1994.
Jacobs, Tod. Telephone conversation, December 7, 1994.

Kohut, Andrew. Telephone conversation, September 29, 1994.

Kavenik, Frank. Telephone conversation, August 2, 1994.

LaPier, David. Telephone conversation, October 4, 1994.

Lonnie, Kevin. Telephone conversation, December 9, 1994.

Mitchell, Duke. Telephone conversation, August 4, 1994.

Pesanelli, David. Telephone conversation, January 25, 1994.

Solomon, Perry. Telephone conversation, July 13, 1994.

Wamble, Marvin. Telephone conversation, October 7, 1994.

Wass, Dudley. Telephone conversation, December 2, 1994.

Wehrfritz, Amy. Telephone conversation, December 5, 1994.

Worden, James. Telephone conversation, December 6, 1994.

Zachmann, William. Telephone conversation, October 17, 1994.

# INDEX

*Italic* page numbers indicate illustrations or captions.
Page numbers followed by a "g" indicate glossary terms.

Dataquest, Inc. 15
data superhighway *see* information superhighway
data visualization 35
DDB Needham Worldwide, Inc. 87–88
Deemer, Candy 87
Deicke Center for Visual Rehabilitation 48
Delorme Mapping Company 13
Delphi Internet Services 93
department stores *98*
design *see* art and design
Design & Build Your Deck (software) 64
DiCiara, Robert 62, 64
Dick Tracy (cartoon character) 7
Digital Directory Assistance 13
digital information transmission 114g
Digital Satellite System (DSS) 101–102
disabled people 47–50, *48*
disk drive 114g
distance learning 115g
Doom (computer game) 18
"downsizing" 36, 45
Droegemueller, Lee 40
Drombrowski, Todd 7–8, 10
Duncan, Richard 94

**E**

EBS Public Relations 22
Eichenberger, Jean 28
Eighty Eight LSS (automobile) 72
Elastic Reality (software) 53
electric-vehicle batteries 75
electric vehicles *74,* 75–76
"electronic agents" 54
Electronic Frontier Foundation 107
electronic mail *see* E-Mail
"electronic shopping malls" 99
E-Mail (electronic mail) 5, 13, 14, 115g

employment 37, 43, *111*
Ernst & Young (accounting firm) 18
Etak, Inc. 71
Excel (software) 24

**F**

FAA *see* Federal Aviation Administration
Face, Sally C. 52
facsimile transmission *see* fax
Fannie Mae (home mortgage organization) 44, 45
farming 35
FasTrak (job-hunting service) 45
fax (facsimile transmission) *x,* 5, 14–15, *15,* 20, 23, 115g
fax/modem 22
FBI *see* Federal Bureau of Investigation
FCC *see* Federal Communications Commission
fear of computers 4
Federal Aviation Administration (FAA) 61
Federal Bureau of Investigation (FBI) 84
Federal Communications Commission (FCC) 103
fiber-optic cable 115g
Fitch, Sandy 40
Fodor's (travel guide series) 71
Folio Corporation 109
Ford Motor Company 73
*Fortune* (magazine) 39
Fox, Ronnie 7
France vi
French, Gary 84–85
Friedman, Joel 79
*Futurist, The* (magazine) 34

**G**

Germany vi

United Air Lines  56, 59
Universal Automatic Computer (UNI-VAC)  11
U.S. Bank Corporation  79
utility plants  34

## V

Value Vision International  98
Veterans Administration  47
video cameras  86
videoconferencing  8–9, 10, 34
video games  60
"Video Reports"  88
Video Toaster (video-editing system)
  *67, 68,* 68–70, 89
Virgin Atlantic Airways  59–60
"virtual corporation"  110–113
"virtual offices"  18
"virtual pharmacy"  10
virtual reality  34, 118g
Visio Home (software)  64
*Vistium* (videoconferencing system)
  28
Visual Research Communications
  (VRC)  88
voice-activated word processing  49
voice-recognition systems  49
*VoiceSpan Modem*  29, *29*
VRC  *see* Visual Research Communications

## W

Wamble, Marvin  27–28
WAN (wide-area network)  118g
*Washington Post* (newspaper)  93
Wass, Dudley C.  73–74
White House (Washington, D.C.)  19
Wichita, Kansas  58
widescreen (letterbox) (TV format)
  118g
Winter Olympic Games (1994) (Lillehammer, Norway)  82–84
*Wired* (magazine)  95
wiretapping  105–106, 107
Wisconsin, University of (Madison)
  75
Word (software)  24
Worden, James  75–76
WordPerfect (software)  22
WordPerfect Office 4.0 (software)  23
word processing  25, 49, 118g
World Trade Center bombing (New
  York City, 1993)  62
World-Wide Web  90
Wright, Benjamin  35

## X

Xerox Corporation  113

## Y

Young & Rubicam (advertising
  agency)  55